FREEDOM
OF RELIGION

Other books in this series:

FREEDOM
OF RELIGION

Edited by Gary Zacharias

Bruce Glassman, *Vice President*
Bonnie Szumski, *Publisher*
Helen Cothran, *Managing Editor*
Scott Barbour, *Series Editor*

GREENHAVEN PRESS
An imprint of Thomson Gale, a part of The Thomson Corporation

THOMSON
GALE

Detroit • New York • San Francisco • San Diego • New Haven, Conn.
Waterville, Maine • London • Munich

© 2005 by Greenhaven Press, a part of The Thomson Corporation.

Thomson and Star Logo are trademarks and Gale and Greenhaven Press are registered trademarks used herein under license.

For more information, contact
Greenhaven Press
27500 Drake Rd.
Farmington Hills, MI 48331-3535
Or you can visit our Internet site at http://www.gale.com

Cover credit: © Bettmann/CORBIS. First graders share a moment of silent prayer at a South Carolina elementary school in 1966.
Library of Congress, 13

LIBRARY OF CONGRESS CATALOGING-IN-PUBLICATION DATA

Freedom of religion / Gary Zacharias, book editor.
  p. cm. — (The Bill of Rights)
Includes bibliographical references and index.
ISBN 0-7377-2647-4 (lib. : alk. paper)
  1. Freedom of religion—United States. 2. Freedom of religion—History.
I. Zacharias, Gary. II. Bill of Rights (San Diego, Calif.)

KF4783.F74 2005
342.7308'52—dc22   2004046074

Printed in the United States of America

exercise one's religion. As a result, it has set
up and occasionally has changed its standards
for judging cases.

2. The Government May Restrict Religious Practice

In 1878 the Supreme Court, in *Reynolds v.
United States*, decided there were occasions
when the government could limit religious
freedom, especially when these practices could
lead to antisocial behavior.

3. No Child May Be Coerced into Saying a Flag Pledge

The Supreme Court ruled in the *West Virginia
State Board of Education v. Barnette* case (1945)
that no national orthodoxy could be forced on
children. Compulsion is not a way to obtain
national unity.

Chapter 4: Perspectives on Religious Freedom in America

1. The Separation of Church and State Is Beneficial to Religion

Many Americans are upset by court cases that
appear to push God and state further apart, but
the separation can be seen as a blessing for
religion in various ways.

2. The Supreme Court's Decisions on the Separation of Church and State Are Flawed

The Supreme Court has misinterpreted Thomas
Jefferson's conception of a "wall of separation
between church and state." As a result, a person's
right to practice his or her religion in public is
being curtailed.

*"I cannot agree with those who think of the Bill of Rights
as an 18th Century straightjacket, unsuited for this age.
. . . The evils it guards against are not only old, they are
with us now, they exist today."*
> —Hugo Black, associate justice of the
> U.S. Supreme Court, 1937–1971

The Bill of Rights codifies the freedoms most essential to American democracy. Freedom of speech, freedom of religion, the right to bear arms, the right to a trial by a jury of one's peers, the right to be free from cruel and unusual punishment—these are just a few of the liberties that the Founding Fathers thought it necessary to spell out in the first ten amendments to the U.S. Constitution.

While the document itself is quite short (consisting of fewer than five hundred words), and while the liberties it protects often seem straightforward, the Bill of Rights has been a source of debate ever since its creation. Throughout American history, the rights the document protects have been tested and reinterpreted. Again and again, individuals perceiving violations of their rights have sought redress in the courts. The courts in turn have struggled to decipher the original intent of the founders as well as the need to accommodate changing societal norms and values.

The ultimate responsibility for addressing these claims has fallen to the U.S. Supreme Court. As the highest court in the nation, it is the Supreme Court's role to interpret the Constitution. The Court has considered numerous cases in which people have accused government of impinging on their rights. In the process, the Court has established a body of case law and precedents that have, in a sense, defined the Bill of Rights. In doing so, the Court has often reversed itself and introduced new ideas and approaches that have altered the legal meaning of the rights contained in the Bill of Rights. As a general rule, the Court has erred on the side of caution, upholding and expanding the rights of individuals rather than restricting them.

An example of this trend is the definition of cruel and unusual punishment. The Eighth Amendment specifically states, "Excessive bail shall not be required, nor excessive fines imposed, nor cruel and unusual punishments inflicted." However, over the years the Court has had to grapple with defining what constitutes "cruel and unusual punishment." In colonial America, punishments for crimes included branding, the lopping off of ears, and whipping. Indeed, these punishments were considered lawful at the time the Bill of Rights was written. Obviously, none of these punishments are legal today. In order to justify outlawing certain types of punishment that are deemed repugnant by the majority of citizens, the Court has ruled that it must consider the prevailing opinion of the masses when making such decisions. In overturning the punishment of a man stripped of his citizenship, the Court stated in 1958 that it must rely on society's "evolving standards of decency" when determining what constitutes cruel and unusual punishment. Thus the definition of cruel and unusual is not frozen to include only the types of punishment that were illegal at the time of the framing of the Bill of Rights; specific modes of punishment can be rejected as society deems them unjust.

Another way that the Courts have interpreted the Bill of Rights to expand individual liberties is through the process of "incorporation." Prior to the passage of the Fourteenth Amendment, the Bill of Rights was thought to prevent only the federal government from infringing on the rights listed in the document. However, the Fourteenth Amendment, which was passed in the wake of the Civil War, includes the words, ". . . nor shall any state deprive any person of life, liberty, or property, without due process of law; nor deny to any person within its jurisdiction the equal protection of the laws." Citing this passage, the Court has ruled that many of the liberties contained in the Bill of Rights apply to state and local governments as well as the federal government. This process of incorporation laid the legal foundation for the civil rights movement—most specifically the 1954 *Brown v. Board of Education* ruling that put an end to legalized segregation.

As these examples reveal, the Bill of Rights is not static. It truly is a living document that is constantly being reinterpreted and redefined. The Bill of Rights series captures this vital aspect of one of America's most cherished founding texts. Each volume in the series focuses on one particular right protected in the Bill of Rights. Through the use of primary and secondary sources, the right's evolution is traced from colonial times to the present. Primary sources include landmark Supreme Court rulings, speeches by prominent experts, and editorials. Secondary sources include historical analyses, law journal articles, book excerpts, and magazine articles. Each book also includes several features to facilitate research, including a bibliography, an annotated table of contents, an annotated list of relevant Supreme Court cases, an introduction, and an index. These elements help to make the Bill of Rights series a fascinating and useful tool for examining the fundamental liberties of American democracy.

The First Amendment to the U.S. Constitution begins with these words: "Congress shall make no law respecting an establishment of religion, or prohibiting the free exercise thereof." These two clauses are short and simply written. The first, commonly called the establishment clause, forbids the federal government from setting up an official state religion in the United States. The second statement, called the free-exercise clause, prevents the federal government from interfering with religious practices of its citizens. Despite the simplicity of these clauses, however, the tension between them has presented a dilemma for the U.S. Supreme Court over the years when it has had to decide on religious freedom issues. As constitutional law attorney Darien A. McWhirter states: "If the Court goes too far to prevent the 'establishment of religion,' it risks interfering with the free exercise of religion, which violates the Free-Exercise Clause. On the other hand, if the Court goes too far to protect the right of free exercise of religion, that might be seen as an attempt to aid one religion or all religions, which would violate the Establishment Clause."[1] In short, the Court has had to protect the people's right to practice their religion without sanctioning any particular religion over another and while maintaining the secular nature of the nation's public institutions.

Nowhere has this tension between the establishment and free-exercise clauses been more evident than in the area of education. Many school districts at one time allowed religious teachers to come into the public schools once a week to provide religious instruction. Many parents and educators supported this practice. However, others believed that the use of public school property, paid for by the entire community, for religious purposes violated the First Amendment because it effectively established a religion. The Supreme Court agreed with these opponents in *McCollum v. Board of Education*

(1948). On the other hand, the Court ruled for the practice of "released time," in which a state would allow students attending public school to be released to receive religious instruction away from the public school. In *Zorach v. Clauson* (1952) the Court argued that this policy avoided excessive entanglement between school and church since it did not use public funds or public buildings. The majority believed a balance could be struck between the establishment and free-exercise clauses. In their opinion, the state could be viewed as accommodating religion rather than supporting religion.

Flag Salutes and Bible Readings

In addition to challenges to religious instruction in schools, mandatory flag salutes in public schools have also been challenged on First Amendment grounds. For some religious groups, like the Jehovah's Witnesses, saluting a flag represents idolatry, an attempt to worship something besides God. The Court had a hard time reaching a decision on this issue. It first ruled in *Minersville School District v. Gobitis* (1940)

Students at a Norfolk, Virginia, elementary school recite the pledge of allegiance in 1941.

that the flag ritual was not a religious rite and that "the flag is the symbol of our national unity, transcending all international differences, however large, within the framework of the Constitution."[2] However, just three years later in *West Virginia State Board of Education v. Barnette* the Court found in favor of the Jehovah's Witnesses by claiming that "no official, high or petty, can prescribe what shall be orthodoxy in politics, nationalism, religion, or other matters of opinion or force citizens to confess by word or act their faith therein."[3] In other words, government cannot command citizens to participate in rituals or profess particular beliefs because to do so is an establishment of religion in violation of the First Amendment.

Bible readings in public schools represent another area of controversy. Many public schools required students to read from the Bible. For example, Maryland law mandated that all public schools in the state start each day with either the reading of a chapter in the Bible or the reciting of the Lord's Prayer. Madalyn Murray, an atheist, complained that this use of the Bible interfered with her son's First Amendment rights because it preferred religious belief over nonbelief. The state argued the readings promoted moral values, taught literature, and perpetuated American institutions. The Court, which combined the Murray case with another case in *Abington Township v. Schempp* (1963), declared the policy to be unconstitutional. The Court said that the state had chosen religious means to accomplish its alleged secular purposes, contrary to the establishment clause. This decision caused an uproar in the country. Since then courts have ruled that the Bible may be taught in literature classes but not in theology classes.

School Prayer

Along with the debate over reading from the Bible, a controversy has arisen over whether and how students may pray in school. A famous case dealing with prayer and school, *Engel v. Vitale*, reached the Supreme Court in 1962. New York State had a voluntary prayer of twenty-two words that students could say as part of opening exercises for the day. Even though this prayer was voluntary and considered nonsectarian, the Court believed it was an infringement of the establishment clause. The chief justice, Hugo Black, stressed in his majority opinion that the Court was not demonstrating a hostility toward religion or prayer. Instead, he warned that government "should stay out of the business of writing or sanctioning official prayers." Prayer in school is a protected right of free speech, but the Court has ruled it has to be done by an individual, not led by the state.

Prayers at public school graduation ceremonies are another area of controversy. In 1992 the case of *Lee v. Weisman* came before the Court. This case involved a school in Middletown, Rhode Island, which allowed a short prayer at the beginning and at the end of the school's public graduation ceremony. As Darien A. McWhirter notes, "The Court had to decide whether this short prayer was like the prayers recited to open legislative sessions (merely a formality that no one really pays any attention to), or like the daily prayers in public school in front of impressionable schoolchildren (which carry the message that the government supports a particular religion)."[4] By a 5-4 ruling, the Court decided that since this ceremony was part of an official public school event, prayers could not be allowed.

Despite the restrictions imposed by the Court, religious activity is not entirely prohibited inside public schools. The Equal Access Act says that if any noncurricular group is allowed to be on school property outside of instructional hours, then all noncurricular groups, including religious ones, must be granted permission. For example, if the stamp club is allowed to meet at a local high school at three o'clock when school is out, then a religious campus group is also allowed to use school facilities for their religious meetings. The same reasoning applies to the annual, student-led "See You at the Pole" meetings that occur in front of the schools before they open in the morning.

Religious instruction, Bible reading, and prayer are not the only practices that generate debate over the place of religion in public schools. The tension between free-exercise and establishment clauses arises in science classes when the topic turns to theories on the origin of the human race. Ever since Darwin promoted his theory of evolution, a debate has raged between those who believe that humans evolved from lower life forms and those who believe humans were created by God. The famous *Scopes* trial in Tennessee (1925) brought this issue to national prominence. John Scopes, a high school biology teacher, was convicted of having violated a law prohibiting the teaching of evolution in public schools. That case, however, did not come to the U.S. Supreme Court. In 1968 a case involving the teaching of evolution made its way to the Supreme Court for the first time; *Epperson v. Arkansas* dealt with an Arkansas law that had prohibited the teaching of the theory of evolution in the public schools as well as universities. The Court decided that Arkansas law violated the establishment clause since it was passed as an attempt to forbid the teaching of a view opposed by certain elements of Christianity.

Public Funding of Private Religious Schools

In addition to the debate over religious exercise in public schools, the Supreme Court also has wrestled with the clash of the establishment and free-exercise clauses as applied to private, sectarian schools. The establishment clause states that Congress cannot "establish" a religion, but most agree that it is also in the state's best interest to provide for all children's education, even if they happen to receive it in religious schools. This issue first came to the Supreme Court in the *Everson v. Board of Education* case (1947), which involved a New Jersey law that stated that parents who sent their children to public or Catholic school could receive a reimbursement from the state for any money spent on bus fare. The state's argument was that it would be less expensive to help pay the bus fare than to build more public schools to house the students if they could not go to their Catholic schools. The Supreme Court, in a 5-4 decision, held that this New Jersey practice was not a violation of the First Amendment and did not establish a religion. The same arguments about the relationship between the state and religious schools have appeared in cases regarding textbooks, vouchers, testing, and therapy. In all these cases the states have argued that it is cost-effective and produces better future citizens to loan textbooks, provide testing and therapy, and give vouchers to parents to pay for a child's education at a school of the parents' choice.

Courts have not ruled consistently on these attempts to use public money for religious schools; they have struggled to come up with a formula to identify how much state money can be given to private school pupils. As Ira Glasser, former executive director of the American Civil Liberties Union, says, "Establishing a clear, principal basis for distinguishing all these religious-school cases is not easy. The Supreme Court's legal theories have hardly been models of clarity or coherence, and many aspects of these decisions are mutually inconsistent."[5] Since the late 1960s the general trend has been toward providing at least some public funds for particular expenses of religious schools.

The two simply worded clauses of the First Amendment, the establishment clause and the free-exercise clause, have created many difficulties for the Supreme Court because of their inherent contradictory messages. Despite the ambiguities of the amendment's wording, and the Court's flip-flop decisions, the basic principle of the separation of church and state in America has worked well. The nation has gained more religious freedom than other countries and has suffered less from religious strife. The education system struggles with some success to provide a secular experience to its students without excluding the religious aspects of society that have been so useful in developing a moral people.

Notes

1. Darien A. McWhirter, *The Separation of Church and State*. Phoenix: Oryx, 1994, p. 4.

2. Quoted in Alvin Johnson and Frank Yost, *Separation of Church and State*. Minneapolis: University of Minnesota Press, 1948, p. 175.

3. Quoted in Patricia Hinchey, *Student Rights*. Santa Barbara, CA: ABC-CLIO, 2001, p. 93.

4. McWhirter, *The Separation of Church and State*, p. 18.

5. Ira Glasser, *Visions of Liberty*. New York: Arcade, 1991, p. 98.

CHAPTER ONE

The Early History of Religious Rights

The Bill of Rights

The Development of Church/State Separatism

Ronald B. Flowers

In the following excerpt Ronald B. Flowers, a recently re-
tired professor of religion and chair of the Department of Religion at Texas Christian University and coauthor of *Toward
Benevolent Neutrality: Church, State, and the Supreme
Court*, traces the change in attitude regarding religious liberties and their connection with the politics of the state in
Western civilization. In the fourth century, Christianity became the established religion of the Roman Empire. For centuries Catholicism was the established religion, according
to Flowers, and church and state worked together. Even
after the Protestant Reformation weakened the Catholic
hold on Europe, the Western world continued to have a close
church/state connection, although different churches were
established as official by different states. English church/state
relations affected the early colonies of North America; some
colonies emulated the relationship that had existed in England, but others, such as Rhode Island and Pennsylvania,
allowed more religious liberty. Finally, the author explains
how churches were gradually pulled away from tight con-
nections to various state governments through several influences, including pluralism, religious revivalism, pietism,
and rationalism.

Christianity became the official religion of the Roman
Empire in the fourth century. In the language of church-
state relations, it became the "established" religion. . . . "Establishment" means an official, formal, symbiotic relationship

between religion and the civil authority. This relationship was assumed to be good for both the state and the church in those early days. It was beneficial for the state in that the moral precepts taught by the church provided an ideology and moral basis for government. It was good for the church, in that it provided the church with political status and influence, protection from competition, and, in some eras, financial assistance from tax monies collected by the state for the benefit of the church.

The arrangement persisted for centuries in the Western world; the Catholic Church was the established church. One might think that when the Protestant Reformers broke with the Roman church, they would also have abandoned its concept of establishment. But that was not the case. Because everyone was so immersed in the idea that it was necessary to have an establishment in order to have a stable political order, the new Protestant movements continued the practice. Even though, with the proliferation of religious movements, church-state alignments became enormously more complicated, the principle and practice of establishment persisted in Western Europe. The most prominent early examples were the Lutheran state churches in Germany and, later, Scandinavia, Henry VIII's Church of England (Anglican), and the established Reformed churches in Huldreich Zwingli's Zurich and John Calvin's Geneva. There is one exception to this generalization: the Anabaptists believed that the civil authority should have nothing to do with matters of religion. But this idea was regarded as heretical by the majority and was a major reason the Anabaptists were persecuted as they were.

Because everything was complicated by the multiplicity of religious groups, in 1555 a treaty was signed, the Peace of Augsburg, which set forth, for Germany, the principle of *cujus regio, ejus religio*, "whose the rule, his or hers the religion." The actual phrase was not used until 1648, in the treaty called the Peace of Westphalia, which expanded the principle to apply to all of Europe. Under this principle, the ruler of a territory had the right to determine the religion of that territory.

The relevance of this for the American situation is that this proestablishment philosophy and this operating principle, "whose the rule, his or hers the religion," were transported to the New World with its earliest permanent settlers.

English Church-State Relations

It is frequently said that the founders of the first American colonies came to the New World for religious freedom. That is not entirely accurate. The earliest of the permanent settlers were those who created the colony of Virginia. They were members of the Anglican Church, which was the established church in England at the time. As such, in England they were not persecuted or otherwise disadvantaged because of their religion. They came to the New World at least as much for its adventure and economic potential as out of missionary zeal. When they created a government for the Virginia colony, they established the Anglican Church; it was to be the only church in the colony. In the traditional style of an establishment, clergy were provided public support in the forms of money or, more often, land and tobacco. "Dale's laws" (1610), named after one of the first governors of the colony, required attendance at Anglican worship by all the citizens of the colony, and persistent violation of the law carried the death penalty. There were also laws against blasphemy and criticism of the Anglican Church or any of its particular doctrines. Again, depending on the seriousness of the profanity, penalties could range from mutilation of one's tongue to death. There is no clear evidence that the laws were rigorously enforced or that the ultimate penalties were ever inflicted. But it is clear that there was no religious freedom in early Virginia. Anglicanism was also at least nominally established in North and South Carolina, Georgia, and, in the eighteenth century, Maryland and New York.

There were in England, however, some people who did not conform to the Church of England. Although they disagreed among themselves about the extent to which they should separate from the national church, they agreed that it should be purified of what they considered to be the residue of Roman Catholicism within it—thus the name "Puritans." When it became clear that the Anglican Church would not follow their admonitions on the purification of the church and that they might lose their wealth or even their lives if they persisted in their criticism, they left for the New World.

Some of the Puritans landed at what is now Plymouth, Massachusetts, in 1620 and a larger group at Massachusetts Bay in 1628. Here they attempted to create the ideal church and state, a commonwealth based on the Bible, . . . an establishment. Because of the form of church government they followed, their church was called "Congregationalist." Puritan laws compelled the observance of Congregationalist faith and practice by all the citizens of the colony. They wanted to keep their religion pure. As one early leader, Nathaniel Ward, said, after naming a list of unacceptable religions, they "shall have free Liberty to keep away from us, and such as will come to be gone as fast as they can, the sooner the better." Did the Puritans mean that? Yes; dissenters were often tried and physically punished, sometimes banished from the colony. Between 1659 and 1661 four Quakers were executed by hanging, including Mary Dyer, the first woman martyr for religious liberty in the New World. In short, these Puritans came to America for religious liberty, but when they got here they created an establishment just as repressive as that from which they had escaped. . . . The Congregationalist church was also established in Connecticut and New Hampshire.

Attempts at Disestablishment

There were exceptions to the pattern of establishment. The most notable were Rhode Island and Pennsylvania. The former was founded by Roger Williams, the most vigorous advocate for religious freedom in the colonial period. He was concerned for the purity of the church and the spiritual welfare of those within it. To preserve that purity, he believed, the church should be separated from the corrupting influences of the state and the "natural man." Consequently, he founded Rhode Island in 1636 on the principle of religious liberty, and the colony became a haven of freedom for those who were persecuted for their religion in other colonies.

Pennsylvania was founded in 1682 by William Penn, a Quaker. The Quakers believed in the concept of the "inner light," something of God in each person, which both sanctified human life and potentially revealed God to the individual. Because one's experience with God could be direct and immediate and persons could understand the inner light differently, the Quakers believed that religion should be free of state-imposed uniformity in thought or practice. However, even in Pennsylvania, political office was available to Christians only. In spite of that restriction, Penn's "Holy Experiment" granted the broadest religious freedom in colonial America.

"Whose the rule, his or hers the religion." That principle was dominant in the early seventeenth century. Most governments chose to try to enforce religious uniformity and exclusivism, although the denominations differed from colony to colony. But others were willing to accommodate religious diversity. In any case, the shape of religion in a colony was dependent on the beliefs of those in power. However, as time progressed, a number of factors emerged to change this situation.

The Role of Pluralism in Separating Church and State

Pluralism is one of the principal features of American religion. "Pluralism" means that in this country we have a multiplicity of religions, each of which thinks of itself as being different enough from others to merit separate existence. It has been that way from the country's beginning. Consequently, it may be artificial to introduce the concept of pluralism under the heading of the eighteenth century, for, as the seventeenth progressed, Dutch Reformed, Lutherans, Roman Catholics, Jews, Baptists, and many nonbelievers journeyed to America. In the eighteenth century, pluralism increased as groups such as the Presbyterians, Mennonites, German Reformed, and Moravians began to arrive in numbers.

My point is that with the increasing diversity of the population it became more difficult for any government to maintain religious homogeneity within its borders. Thus one of the traditional arguments for an establishment, a stable political order based on an official theology and set of moral ideas, became progressively irrelevant. In addition, Rhode Island and Pennsylvania, which were flourishing, demonstrated that it was possible to have orderly government and a stable society even without religious uniformity. They were successful "laboratory schools" of religious pluralism.

Furthermore, from the perspective of the various religious groups, there was a very practical implication of this pluralism. None of them was large enough or powerful enough to become the dominant, much less the sole, religious group in an area. Each decided that if it could not have that kind of power for itself, it did not want any other group to have it either. Stated differently, groups perceived that if any one group was given political power, all others would be disadvantaged. Better that all religious groups be equal before the law. So pluralism was one of several factors in the eighteenth century that contributed to the eventual separation of church and state in America.

Religious Revivals Ironically Separate Church and State

Beginning in the 1720s with regional outbursts and reaching its peak from 1740 to 1742, the Great Awakening contributed significantly to the process of disestablishment. The Great Awakening was a revival movement that swept the eastern seaboard, spread primarily by the enormously talented preacher George Whitefield. The revival sought to enliven the churches, which many religious leaders saw as spiritually dead or at least in the doldrums, by preaching a message of spiritual renewal and discipline. It was not enough to be a lukewarm Christian; one should know that he or she was a sinful creature, estranged from God, before receiving God's forgiveness. But, by God's grace, salvation and spiritual revitalization were available. Much of this preaching was done not in churches, but in open-air meetings, thus reaching large crowds. Many people had conversion experiences. It is difficult to know how many conversions there were; eighteenth-century preachers were not much better at accurately reporting such numbers than modern ones. But historians are convinced that the churches of various denominations were revitalized and enlarged by the Great Awakening.

Historically it had been argued that it was necessary to have an establishment to get people into the churches; the police power of the state would be used to compel people to attend worship. . . . But those who responded to the revival preachers did so voluntarily, because they were attracted to the gospel. There was no coercion, yet people came to listen to preachers, worship, and join churches. Some began to wonder why, if it was possible to attract people to religion and churches through persuasion, it was necessary to continue the establishment pattern? Such thinking later contributed to the formulation of the concept of separation of church and state.

Theology Itself Led to Disestablishment

In addition to the persuasive power of orthodox Christian preaching, many people at the time drew antiestablishment conclusions from the theology itself: Human beings are sinful; their stiff-necked pride causes them to rebel against God, thus distorting, if not destroying, the relationship between humans and God that God originally intended. This sin manifests itself in all sorts of ways, from minor peccadilloes to deeds of abject evil. Human beings cannot restore this relationship with God themselves. God, in an act of ultimate mercy, sent Jesus Christ to be the savior of humankind.

Those who heard this good news and in whom God ignited faith (Calvinist) or who responded to the message (Arminian) were brought into a restored relationship with God; they were Christian. But this was an individual experience. Without discounting the church as the place where the gospel was rightly preached and the sacraments rightly administered, as the community of the faithful gathered for mutual support and spiritual nurture, nonetheless the experience of salvation was ultimately an individual experience.

In the American environment, some began to make a connection between the personal experience of salvation and political religious freedom. The experience of becoming Christian was dependent on the work of the Holy Spirit within one, not the theological dictates of a state-controlled church. The liberating experience of salvation meant freedom from the "principalities and powers," not only from sin, but the political powers as well. Furthermore, there was no guarantee that all should respond to the call of God in the same way. . . .

An Emphasis on Reason

Another contributor to eventual separation was the opposite of pietism: rationalism. In this age of the Enlightenment, many became convinced of the virtual invincibility of human reason. Reason could perceive and understand all that was worth knowing; it could formulate ethical principles; it could devise systems of government. There was great emphasis on the worth and abilities of human beings. Rationalists were not unanimous in their views of religion. Some said that reason took the place of God: by relying on reason, humans no longer had need for God; religion was only antiquated superstition. Others took the position that reason could demonstrate the existence of God; for example, the complexity and precision of the universe implied the existence of a Designer. This theistic form of rationalism was known as Deism and was the position of many of those great men who were responsible for writing the Constitution. Their Deism greatly influenced their views of church-state relationships. They were convinced that any institution that hindered reason, interfered with free, creative thought, shackled the minds of men and women, was bad. They knew history well enough to know that the established church had had just such an impact. Theological orthodoxy imposed by law, the medieval Inquisitions, and the heresy trials and executions of the American colonies taught them that an established church was inimical to political and intellectual freedom. Consequently, they were not willing to make establishment a characteristic of the new nation they were creating.

How Virginia Was a Model

In sum, a variety of factors, practical, theological, and philosophical, contributed to constitutional disestablishment. A final factor was the almost laboratory experience of Virginia. By 1779 Virginia had become as religiously pluralistic as the other colonies and many of its inhabitants were rethinking church-state relationships. The Anglican establishment was considerably weakened.

In 1784 a taxation bill was introduced in the Virginia legislature that was intended for the support of the Christian religion rather than any particular sect. The tax was to be collected by the civil authorities, but the taxpayer could designate which Christian group would receive the money. If one chose no Christian organization to receive the tax, it would go to education. The principal sponsor of the bill was Patrick Henry, who argued that governmental support of religion was necessary in order to have a moral society. The principal opponent of the bill was James Madison, who expressed his opposition in a document entitled "Memorial and Remonstrance against Religious Assessments." Madison marshaled rationalistic and philosophical arguments against any tax bill whatsoever, in the process making the case for religious freedom in a variety of forceful ways. No document has argued for religious freedom more eloquently: it is an American classic.

Madison's purpose in writing the piece was to sway public opinion against the taxation bill. In that he was extraordinarily successful. In 1785 the legislature defeated the taxation bill. Madison took advantage of this moment to reintroduce to the legislature Thomas Jefferson's "Bill for Establishing Religious Freedom." Jefferson had first introduced this bill in 1779, and it had been tabled by the legislature every year since. But now, in the climate created by the "Memorial and Remonstrance," the bill was enacted into law in January 1786. The importance of these events is not only that Virginia became a trailblazer in the American movement toward the separation of church and state, but also that it gave Madison the opportunity to crystallize and articulate his thoughts on the question of religious liberty before he went to Philadelphia to work on the Constitution, to which we now turn.

The Constitution

When the statesmen who founded this country wrote the Constitution, they mentioned religion in only one place, Article VI. What they wrote is a prohibition. In Article VI, as a part of the requirement that state and federal officeholders take an oath or make an affirmation to support the Constitution, the founders wrote: "but no religious Test shall ever be required as a Qualification to any Office or public Trust under the United States." There is no reference to God or to any religious tradition in the Constitution. Apparently this was not an oversight.

Does that mean that the founders were hostile to religion or even to Christianity? No, it means that they recognized, given the multiplicity of religions in the new nation and the distressing history of governmental oppression in the name of religion, that it would be better for them to leave the question alone. To avoid getting involved in a quagmire of competing religious loyalties, the government should remain neutral. Furthermore, it was a way of asserting the limited nature of government. The state had no powers that were not enumerated in the Constitution. By not mentioning religion, the founders were not expressing animosity toward religion, but rather keeping the sacred matter of religion from the reach of government. In the words of Madison, the Constitution was not to grant "a shadow of right in the general government to intermeddle with religion." However, since the government obviously needed to set the requirements for public office, the authors addressed themselves to this question. Public office would be independent of religious belief or the lack thereof.

This provision of Article VI did not create the separation of church and state. But it went a long way to minimize in the new nation the possibility of the religious strife and oppression that had been known in the history of the Western world. Apparently the majority of Americans were satisfied with the Constitution's virtual silence on the question of religion, for it was ratified in 1789. But many were not satisfied by the silence of the Constitution on the larger question of the freedoms of citizens, including the freedom of religion. Consequently, the founders drew up a list guaranteeing particular freedoms: the Bill of Rights.

The Constitution Created a Secular Government

John M. Swomley

John M. Swomley is professor emeritus of social ethics at St. Paul School of Theology. He is a member of the national board of the American Civil Liberties Union and has authored many books, including *Religion, the State, and the Schools* and *The Politics of Liberation.*

In the selection that follows, Swomley argues that the U.S. Constitution was clearly intended to create a secular government. To support this claim, he contrasts the language of the Declaration of Independence with that of the Constitution. Unlike the declaration, which contains phrases such as "Nature's God" and "Divine Providence," the Constitution contains only one reference to religion: a clause that prohibits religious tests for office. For the first time a government was set up that established a doctrine of separation of church and state. Although the document did not forbid religion and politics from mixing, it guaranteed people the right to worship any way they felt and protected them from government interference in religious matters. The author concludes that people were not convinced the Constitution would protect their religious rights. As a result, fears of government power led many to call for a bill of rights to keep the federal government from meddling with people's religious beliefs and activities.

T he constitutional doctrine of separation of church and state is a uniquely American contribution to government. It means that government has no authority to invade the field of religion, that government agencies may neither advance nor inhibit religion, and that government may not take account of a person's religion or lack of it in determining qualification for holding public office or for government employment. The only function of government with respect to religion is that of protecting the right of conscience, worship, autonomous control over doctrine, governance and resources of religious groups, and the private and public expression of religious conviction.

Separation of church and state does not mean separation of religion and politics. The religious or nonreligious person or group may freely engage in political speech and action that criticizes or supports government policies. Congress, however, has been able to limit lobbying by churches through the granting of tax exemption and tax deductibility of contributions to nonprofit agencies that use only a fraction of their resources to influence legislation.

The Constitution of the United States provides for a wholly secular government. Any action by the Congress, the Executive, or Judiciary that confers any benefit upon religious organizations or places any impediment in the way of religious expression that does not infringe the rights of others is a violation of the letter and spirit of the Constitution.

The Constitution, wrote the historian Charles A. Beard, "does not confer upon the Federal government any power whatever to deal with religion in any form or manner." James Madison called it "a bill of powers." He said that "the powers are enumerated and it follows that all that are not granted by the Constitution are retained" by the people.

The Constitution as a Contract

The Constitution must be understood as a social contract between the people and the United States. The Tenth Amendment spells out the meaning of the social contract in these words: "The powers not delegated to the United States by the Constitution, nor prohibited by it to the states, are reserved to the states respectively or to the people."

The social contract idea came from the political philosophy of John Locke, who had been a strong influence on many leading Americans, including Thomas Jefferson and James

Madison. Partly under John Locke's influence, Jefferson and Madison came to believe that a government that was formed as a social contract had no power given to it to act on religious matters. Locke, who had popularized the social contract theory of government, asserted in his first *Letter Concerning Toleration* that "the care of souls cannot belong to the civil magistrate because his power consists only in outward force; but true and saving religion consists in the inward persuasion of the mind. . . ."

Locke's statement in modern language is the idea that true religion is a matter of faith and that, if a church cannot persuade its members to accept its doctrine or contribute to its work, it is not the business of government to enforce the faith or pay its expenses. Governor Mario Cuomo of New York in 1984 defended his position of not seeking laws against abortion, following the assertion by Catholic bishops that Catholic politicians could not draw a line between their personal faith and public policy, when he said: "We seem to be in the position of asking government to make criminal what we believe to be sinful because we ourselves can't stop committing the sin."

The secular nature of the Constitution is clearly evident in the only reference to religion in it prior to the adoption of the First Amendment. That reference is in Article VI, Section 3, which forbids religious tests for public office.

Although the Declaration of Independence, produced only eleven years earlier, contains various religious terms such as "Nature's God," the "Supreme Judge of the world," and "Divine Providence," the Constitution has no such reference. It refers incidentally to religion in that Sundays are not to be counted in the number of days within which the president may veto legislation. This absence of religious references does not reflect any hostility to religion or even imply its unimportance. Rather, it is a recognition that religion would thrive better if left uninfluenced, unaided, and unimpeded by government.

Separation of Church and State in the Constitution

Article VI, Section 3, which is the first specific statement of separation of church and state other than the secular nature of the Constitution itself, says:

The Senators and Representatives before mentioned, and the members of the several State Legislatures, and all executive and judicial officers both of the United States and of the several States, shall be bound by oath or affirmation to support this Constitution; but no religious test shall ever be required as a qualification to any office or public trust under the United States.

This section is significant not only because it permitted any person without regard to religion to hold public office, but also because it provided for the use of "affirmation" as an alternative to a religious oath. An affirmation was understood as a solemn declaration by a person conscientiously opposed to taking an oath but which is parallel to the religious oath in value and penalty if violated.

The impact of this section of the Constitution has been of major significance to religious liberty. In itself it was an important impediment to the establishment or government support of any church. One reason for this is that the unchurched as well as adherents of churches dissenting to establishment were numerically larger than the combined memberships of all the churches that were formerly established during the colonial era or of those that could have had aspirations of such support at the time the Constitution was adopted.

Anson Phelps Stokes, in his monumental work *Church and State in the United States*, wrote that "Congress as constituted with men and women from all the denominations could never unite in selecting any one body" as an established church. "This has been so evident from the time of the founding of the government that it is one reason why the First Amendment must be interpreted more broadly than merely as preventing the state establishment of religion which had already been made almost impossible."

Comments by the Framers of the Constitution

Stokes's statement is supported by comments made by contemporaries of the framing of the Constitution. Oliver Ellsworth, a member of the Continental Congress from Connecticut, a delegate to the Constitutional Convention, and the third Chief Justice of the United States Supreme Court, noted in one of his writings that in European nations with established churches there were always religious tests for holding office. Edmund Randolph, a delegate to the Constitutional Convention and the first Attorney General of the United States, referred to "no religious" tests for public office as meaning that those in office "are not bound to support one mode of worship or to adhere to one particular sect." Therefore, given the variety of religious organizations in the United States, "they will prevent the establishment of any one sect, in prejudice to the rest and forever oppose all attempts to infringe religious liberty."

James Iredell, a Supreme Court Justice from 1790 to 1799, who served in the North Carolina Convention that ratified the Constitution, referred to the exclusion of a religious test for public office as one way to establish religious liberty. He said that Congress had no power to create "the establishment of any religion whatsoever; and I am astonished that any gentleman should conceive that they have. . . . If any future Congress should pass an act concerning the religion of the country, it would be an act which they are not authorized to pass, by the Constitution. . . ."

Another North Carolinian, Richard Dobbs Spaight, who had been a delegate to the Constitutional Convention, said about religion, "No power is given to the general government to interfere with it at all. Any act of Congress on this subject would be a usurpation."

The Need for a Bill of Rights

Although the members of the Constitutional Convention and many other Americans believed that the new federal government had no power to legislate with respect to religion, there were many who feared the usurpation of power. They wanted to have a bill of rights that would effectively prevent the federal government from meddling with religion. Thomas Tredwell of New York opposed ratification of the Constitution, arguing that it needed a bill of rights. He said that he wished that "sufficient caution had been used to secure to us our religious liberties, and to have prevented the general government from tyrannizing over our consciences by a religious establishment—a tyranny of all others most dreadful and which will assuredly be exercised whenever it shall be thought necessary for the promotion and support of their political measures."

Even in Virginia, James Madison and others who favored a federal union could not persuade the state convention to ratify the federal Constitution until it accepted a recommendation for a bill of rights. The opposition to ratification was led by Patrick Henry and George Mason. Mason had been a delegate to the Constitutional Convention in Philadelphia, but had refused to sign the Constitution because it did not have a bill of rights. He had been the principal author in 1776 of Virginia's Declaration of Rights. One of Virginia's proposed amendments to a federal bill of rights stated that "no particular religious sect or society ought to be favored or established by law, in preference to others."

Although Virginia ratified the Constitution, Rhode Island and North Carolina did not do so until after Congress had adopted the Bill of Rights.

The first Congress produced the Bill of Rights, but without the unanimous enthusiasm of all its members. Some members of the Congress opposed the proposal for a bill of rights on the ground that it was unnecessary because the Constitution did not grant the government any power to deal with religion or other rights retained by the people. James Madison originally shared this view. He told the Virginia convention, June 12, 1788, prior to its ratification of the Constitution: "There is not a shadow of right in the general government to intermeddle with religion." Madison, however, felt duty-bound to respect the Virginia convention's recommendation of a bill of rights. He also had come to believe that a bill of rights was needed to make doubly sure that Congress would not exercise powers not granted to it under the Constitution.

The Founders Debated the Church/State Relationship

Walter Berns

Walter Berns is the John M. Olin professor emeritus at Georgetown University and a resident scholar at the American Enterprise Institute, a conservative public policy research organization. He has been a delegate at the UN Commission on Human Rights and has written several books, including *In Defense of Liberal Democracy* and *Making Patriots*.

In the following excerpt Berns describes the creation of the religion clauses of the First Amendment by the first Congress. The Congress agreed that there should be no restrictions on the free exercise of religion and that the federal government should not be allowed to establish a national religion. However, there was some disagreement over whether states should be allowed to establish a religion and whether either states or the federal government should be allowed to aid religions. In the end, according to Berns, the wording of the amendment reflects a compromise between these various factions, an outcome that has resulted in continued debate about the meaning of the establishment clause up to the present.

The Constitution, as it was sent by the Philadelphia convention to the people of the states for their ratification, contained a single provision dealing with religion: the proscription in Article VI of religious tests for office. This did not satisfy the six states (or five states plus the minority in Pennsylvania) that included a demand for a guarantee of the rights

Walter Berns, *The First Amendment and the Future of American Democracy*. New York: Basic Books, Inc., Publishers, 1976. Copyright © 1976 by Basic Books. Reproduced by permission of Basic Books, conveyed through Copyright Clearance Center, Inc.

of conscience in their general call for a bill of rights. The typical demand made by these states was for an amendment protecting freedom of conscience, but no one, ratifier or nonratifier (or, as the nonratifier Elbridge Gerry inelegantly put it, "rats or antirats") expressed an opinion opposed to freedom of conscience. There was simply no debate on the subject, nor even a recorded difference of opinion, and this is not unrelated to the fact that freedom of conscience has not been an issue in the subsequent history of the country. More strikingly, especially to anyone with a memory of British and even American history during the seventeenth and eighteenth centuries, the fact that freedom of conscience was not an issue shows the great extent to which the religious question had already been settled in America at the time the Constitution was being written. There was a debate as to whether an amendment was necessary to protect it, but that posed no serious problem. There was considerable controversy over the question of whether the House should take time from the consideration of the pressing necessity to establish the offices of government in order to honor a pledge (which some of them did not regard as a pledge) to add a bill of rights to the Constitution; but that too proved tractable. The real difference was not discussed at all, although it can be glimpsed in the variety of formulations given the amendment; this was a difference that divided the participants among themselves and divided the more profound of them within themselves. In one sense, they were opposed to religion, to the organized religions of the day; in another sense, they recognized the role religion could play—and perhaps would have to play—in free government. Unlike freedom of conscience, this difference, the ambiguity on this aspect of the religious question, gave rise to an issue that has played a role in the subsequent history of the country and underlies the disagreement concerning the meaning of the First Amendment.

In 1947, for example, the Supreme Court said of the establishment clause that it means that neither a state nor the federal government may set up a church, pass laws aiding one religion or all religions, or prefer one religion over another. This is a view widely held among constitutional schol-

ars, but it is by no means the only view. . . . It was not the
view of the Court when it upheld the statute granting tax exemptions to churches for properties used for worshiping purposes. Presumably, it was not the view of Mr. Justice
[William] Douglas when . . . he wrote that Americans "are a
religious people whose institutions presuppose a Supreme
Being," although it was his view, a few years later, when he
wrote that the purpose of the religious clauses was "to keep
government neutral, not only between sects, but between believers and nonbelievers." Of course, the federal government
may not "set up a church"; there has never been any argument about that. But may it aid religion, provided it does
so on a nondiscriminatory basis? May the states? These
are the questions agitated today, and a good deal depends on
the answers given. Because they are so important, we are
not surprised to learn that they were raised—and answered
—during the debates on the religious clauses in the First
Congress.

The Debates Begin

In the Virginia ratifying convention, Patrick Henry had complained that under the proposed Constitution the states
would lose their sovereignty which would thereby make inse-
cure the rights of conscience protected under the state constitutions and, specifically, under the Virginia constitution.
In response to Henry, and to others who in other states had
expressed similar apprehensions, [James] Madison opened
the debates in the First Congress by proposing an amendment forbidding the establishment of "any national religion"
or the infringement of "the full and equal rights of conscience." The issue here had to do with the relation of nation
and states; but it was not much of an issue. The states had
sought some reassurance, and the Founders had no objection
to providing it. The House Select Committee formulated
Madison's proposal as follows: "no religion shall be established by law, nor shall the equal rights of conscience be infringed." This led Benjamin Huntington of Connecticut to
express the fear that this language could be read—not by him
but by others—to forbid state laws requiring contributions in

support of ministers of religion and places of worship. In addition, although he favored the free exercise of religion, he was anxious, he said, to avoid any language that might "patronize those who professed no religion at all." He too was concerned with the nation-state relationship, but the source of his concern was his desire to allow the states to provide aid to religion.

Samuel Livermore of New Hampshire and Elbridge Gerry of Massachusetts were also intent on preserving their state laws in aid of religion and fostering the public worship of God. Gerry proposed to change the establishment clause to make it read "that no religious doctrine shall be established by law." Livermore, with Gerry's support, wanted to change it to read "that Congress shall make no laws touching religion," which, if adopted (and the House at one point did adopt it by a vote of 31-20), would have prevented national laws "touching" or affecting or regulating or interfering with state laws on the subject of religion, including those laws that could be said to have established religion. Madison's answer to Huntington's fear was the suggestion that the word "national" be "inserted before religion," thus leaving room for these state establishments; but Gerry, for the same reason that had earlier led him to vote against ratification of the Constitution in the Massachusetts ratifying convention, objected to the very use of the word "national."

Madison's amendments, as he had introduced them at the outset of the debates, would have forbidden the states, as well as the federal government, to "violate the equal rights of conscience." This suggests what we know from his other writings to be the case—that he was opposed to state as well as to federal establishment. In fact, he regarded this restriction on the states as "the most valuable amendment in the whole list," a judgment in line with his well-known opinion that the states were much more likely than the federal government to be ruled by factions, which would deprive religious minorities of their rights. This restriction on the states was adopted by the House and was lost only in the Senate.

Finally, on August 20, 1789, the House adopted the amendment in the style proposed by Fisher Ames of Massachusetts:

"Congress shall make no law establishing religion, or to prevent the free exercise thereof, or to infringe the rights of conscience." With insignificant stylistic changes, this is the form in which it was sent to the Senate. The following conclusions may be drawn from the House action: both the state and the federal governments were forbidden to infringe the rights of conscience, and, assuming there was a distinction (the Senate was to see none), the federal government was also forbidden to prevent the free exercise of religion; and the federal government (but not the states) was forbidden to establish religion. But did Ames, Huntington, Gerry, and Livermore, as well as some others, think that the federal government was also being forbidden to aid religion? Although we have no record of their debates, we know from the actions taken that this was made an issue by the Senate.

The Senate Creates a Different Wording

The House amendments were formally read in the Senate on August 25, and, after a debate that was interrupted more than once, the Senate completed its consideration of them on September 9. As mentioned, the single amendment placing restrictions on the states was dropped; the amendment dealing with religion and that dealing with speech and press were combined into one; various changes were made to others; but, on the whole, they were adopted by the Senate in the form in which they came from the House. The establishment clause, however, was the subject of a number of amendments proposed and occasionally adopted. The first of these, offered on September 3, would have forbidden Congress to make any law "establishing one religious sect or society in preference to others" —which is certainly less ambiguous on the meaning of establishment than either the House version or the First Amendment as finally adopted—and it dropped the free exercise clause while retaining that part of the House version prohibiting infringement of the rights of conscience. It was defeated, then accepted; but the acceptance did not have the effect of ending the debate. After defeating a series of proposed changes, the Senate ended the day by returning to the House version, including the free exercise clause, but this time dropping the clause protecting the rights of conscience. From this it would appear that the senators regarded the latter as redundant, and it does not appear again. There continued to be some dissatisfaction with the establishment clause, however, with some senators anxious, and ultimately a majority of senators willing, to be more precise as to what would constitute an establishment. Hence, on September 9, the Senate adopted the following version, and this was the one it sent back to the House: "Congress shall make no law establishing articles of faith, or a mode of worship, or prohibiting the free exercise of religion. . . ." This seemingly would have left intact the various state establishments and would have permitted federal aid to religion on a nondiscriminatory basis. However, since we have no record of what was said in the Senate, we cannot know for certain that this was the intent.

Madison's Role in the Conference

The House refused to accept this version and asked for a conference. The Conference Committee, with Madison one of the House conferees, proposed the amendment in the form that was finally adopted by the required two-thirds vote in each house and ratified by the required three-fourths of the states: "Congress shall make no law respecting an establishment of religion, or prohibiting the free exercise thereof. . . ." Here, then, is the origin of the troublesome phrase "respecting an establishment of religion."

Irving Brant, in his biography of Madison, says "there can be little doubt that this was written by Madison," and that, "of all the versions of the religious guaranty, this most directly covered the thing he was aiming at—absolute separation of church and state and total exclusion of government aid to religion." But this is not altogether accurate. For example, Madison did not succeed in his attempt to place restrictions on the powers of the states with respect to the rights of conscience. Moreover, even if it is true that Madison was the author of this final formulation of the First Amendment, it is not necessarily the case that it was intended to promote the "absolute separation of church and state" or to forbid all forms of governmental aid to religion, even aid from the federal government. After all, this same First Congress, with Madison's approval, readopted the Northwest Ordinance of 1787, first passed by the Continental Congress, the third article of which reads as follows: "Religion, morality, and knowledge, being necessary to good government and the happiness of mankind, schools and the means of learning shall forever be encouraged." It is not easy to see how Congress, or a territorial government acting under the authority of Congress, could promote religious and moral education under a Constitution that promoted "the absolute separation of church and state" and forbade all forms of assistance to religion. Whatever his own views—and we shall turn to those shortly—the situation that prevailed in the country and was reflected in the debates on the First Amendment would have required Madison to accommodate the views of others in whatever formulation he arrived at. The Senate wanted to prohibit federal laws "establishing articles of faith, or a mode of worship"; the House wanted to prohibit federal laws establishing religion; they agreed to the final version prohibiting laws "respecting" *an* establishment of religion. The question concerns the meaning of the words "respecting an establishment of religion."

The House debate had begun on the Select Committee's version of the amendment, which read as follows: "No religion shall be established by law, nor shall the equal rights of conscience be infringed." The debate was opened by Peter Sylvester of New York, who objected to this formulation because "it might be thought to have a tendency to abolish religion altogether." So to construe the clause seems unnecessarily apprehensive—unless Sylvester had reason to believe that to forbid the establishment of religion by law would be to forbid all governmental assistance to religion, and that without this assistance religion would languish and eventually die. What is of interest is Madison's reply:

> Mr. Madison said, he apprehended the meaning of the words to be, that Congress should not establish *a* religion, and enforce the legal observation of it by law, nor compel men to worship God in any manner contrary to their conscience. Whether the words are necessary or

not, he did not mean to say, but they had been required by some of the State conventions, who seemed to entertain an opinion that under the clause of the constitution, which gave power to Congress to make all laws necessary and proper to carry into execution the constitution, and the laws made under it, enabled them to make laws of such a nature as might infringe the rights of conscience, and establish *a* national religion; to prevent these effects he presumed the amendment was intended, and he thought it as well expressed as the nature of the language would admit.

Can the Government Assist Religion?

Madison here twice adds the article—*a* religion—which, as a recent student of the debates has written, had it appeared in the original, would have made it virtually impossible for Sylvester to read the clause as forbidding "nondiscriminatory assistance to religion." By the addition of the article, Madison seems to have expressed a willingness to accommodate those who wanted to permit such assistance. Can this also be said of the phrase "respecting an establishment of religion"? Perhaps; perhaps even probably. There were those who insisted on room for such assistance, and the language permits it. What is beyond question is that both the states and the federal government have traditionally acted as if the language permitted assistance of some sort. "Our system," as Justice Douglas had cause to complain, is "honeycombed" with laws that provide that assistance at both the federal and the state levels. And when he and others insist that this is in violation of the Constitution, which was intended "to keep government neutral, not only between sects, but also between believers and nonbelievers," they are required to look elsewhere for supporting authority—to Madison's "Memorial and Remonstrance," for example. Written in opposition to the Virginia bill "for establishing a provision for teachers of the Christian religion," this famous statement of Madison's own views calls for the separation not only of church and state but of religion and state. But what is clear is that more than Madison's own views went into the First Amendment.

In the past, and especially in that recent English-speaking past well known to the Founders, religion had been the most divisive of political issues, the cause of civil strife and wars, of test oaths and recusancy, of revolutions and regicides, of political problems that threatened to defy solution, of, as Madison put it in the "Memorial and Remonstrance," "torrents of blood" spilled in the vain attempt to "extinguish Religious discord." What is noteworthy in the debates leading to the adoption of the First Amendment is the absence of that kind of religious problem. It is not the differences among the participants in that debate but rather the extent of their agreement that is remarkable. What divided them were differences on what can only, in the light of that history, be called secondary issues: whether government depended in some way on religion and, therefore, whether government should be permitted, in some way, to foster religion, and whether this should be done at the federal as well as the state level. On these questions Madison especially differed from Samuel Livermore and his friends; but even Madison made no attempt in the First Amendment debates to have Congress adopt the policy he favored so eloquently and effectively in his "Memorial and Remonstrance." Compared to these differences, the agreement among them was massive. There was no dispute about freedom of conscience or the free exercise of religion; the adoption of the clause protecting free exercise was an altogether perfunctory matter, giving rise to no difference whatsoever. There was no dispute with respect to the principles on which the Constitution was built; stated in its most radical form, they all agreed that our institutions do *not* presuppose a providential Supreme Being. This is a fact of considerable significance, and . . . it allows us to understand why the Founders distinguished between religious and political opinion, and why they could accord absolute freedom to the one and not to the other.

A Religious People Create a Secular Document

One of the striking facts about the original, unamended Constitution is the absence of any passage invoking the name of God, providing for the public worship of God, according special privileges or places to churchmen, or stating it to be the duty of Congress to promote Christian education as part of a design to promote good citizenship. There is nothing in it similar to the provision in the Massachusetts constitution in 1780 declaring it to be not only the right but also the duty of the "towns, parishes, precincts and other bodies politic" to support, and to provide money for the support of, "the public worship of God." Instead, the Constitution merely makes it possible for legislative majorities to enact—or not enact—laws of this sort. Yet what is regarded as primary or essential is not left to the discretion of legislative majorities or to chance. We have grown so accustomed to what we today call the secular state that we tend to ignore the significance of the absence of such provisions in the federal Constitution. If the Founders had intended to establish a Christian commonwealth (and, under the circumstances, it could not have been any other variety of religious commonwealth), it was remiss of them—indeed, sinful of them—not to have said so and to have acted accordingly. If they thought that all government was derived from God, they would have been remiss in not establishing constitutional institutions calculated to cause or help Americans to live according to His laws. Instead, the first of Madison's amendments, proposed in response to the demands of the states for a bill of rights, was a declaration insisting not that all power derives from God, but "that all power is originally vested in, and consequently derives from, the people." Instead of speaking of men's duties to God and to each other, the Founders spoke—and again in this first of the proposed amendments—of men's indubitable, unalienable, and indefeasible rights, including the right freely to acquire and use property.

All this is not to say that Americans were not, in some sense—in most cases, some subordinate sense—a "religious people." Sylvester, Huntington, Livermore, and Gerry were indeed speaking on behalf of religion, but even their cause was a far cry from the causes defended by religious enthusiasts of the past. Massachusetts did require in its 1780 constitution that men had a duty publicly to worship God—but this was significantly qualified by the concession that each man do this according to "the dictates of his own conscience." What is more, this duty was imposed for a political reason. The towns "and other bodies politic" were to provide support for "the public worship of God" *because* "the happiness of a people, and the good order and preservation of civil government, essentially depend upon piety, religion, and morality." This position was better stated in the Massachusetts ratifying convention when John Turner said that "without the prevalence of Christian piety and morals, the best republican constitution can never save us from slavery and ruin." On the basis of such statements, it might even be said that whereas our institutions do not presuppose a Supreme Being, their preservation does. This is a venerable opinion. [French writer and politician Alexis de] Tocqueville goes so far as to say that it was the opinion of all Americans:

> Indeed, it is in this same point of view that the inhabitants of the United States themselves look upon religious belief. I do not know whether all Americans have a sincere faith in their religion—for who can search the human heart?—but I am certain that they hold it to be indispensable to the maintenance of republican institutions. This opinion is not peculiar to a class of citizens or to a party, but it belongs to the whole nation and to every rank of society.

To some extent, Americans were taught this political lesson by the Founders.

CHAPTER TWO

The Establishment Clause and the Supreme Court

The Bill of Rights

The Challenge of Interpreting the Establishment Clause

Charles Haynes, Oliver Thomas, and John Ferguson

The First Amendment Center, affiliated with Vanderbilt University, works to preserve and protect First Amendment freedoms through information and education. In the following selection, three of its writers describe the difficulty the Supreme Court faces in interpreting the establishment clause. The article explores why the clause has created so many arguments: Some believe it prohibits only the establishment of a single national church, but others claim it prohibits establishment of religion in general.

In order for the Supreme Court to interpret this clause, over the years it has used several tests, including the *Lemon*, coercion, endorsement, and neutrality tests. The first test, referring to the 1971 decision *Lemon v. Kurtzman*, requires the court to determine whether the action in question advances or inhibits religion and whether it excessively entangles religion and government. The coercion test comes from Justice Anthony Kennedy, who suggested the government violates the establishment clause if it aids religion in such a way as to establish a state church or forces people to support religion against their will. A third test, proposed by Justice Sandra Day O'Connor, says the government has established a religion if a reasonable observer would believe the government is either endorsing or disapproving of religion. Finally, under the neutrality test, the government must treat religious groups as it would any other group in the allocation of government funds for public services such as education.

The first of the First Amendment's two religion clauses reads: "Congress shall make no law respecting an establishment of religion. . . ." Note that the clause is absolute. It allows *no* law. It is also noteworthy that the clause forbids more than the establishment of religion by the government. It forbids even laws *respecting* an establishment of religion. The establishment clause sets up a line of demarcation between the functions and operations of the institutions of religion and government in our society. It does so because the framers of the First Amendment recognized that when the roles of the government and religion are intertwined, the result too often has been bloodshed or oppression.

For the first 150 years of our nation's history, there were very few occasions for the courts to interpret the establishment clause because the First Amendment had not yet been applied to the states. As written, the First Amendment applied only to Congress and the federal government. In the wake of the Civil War, however, the 14th Amendment was adopted. It reads in part that "no state shall . . . deprive any person of life, liberty or property without due process of law. . . ." In 1947 the Supreme Court held in *Everson v. Board of Education* that the establishment clause is one of the "liberties" protected by the due-process clause. From that point on, all government action, whether at the federal, state, or local level, must abide by the restrictions of the establishment clause.

Establishment

There is much debate about the meaning of the term "establishment of religion." Although judges rely on history, the framers' other writings and prior judicial precedent, they sometimes disagree. Some, including Chief Justice William Rehnquist, argue that the term was intended to prohibit only the establishment of a single national church or the preference of one religious sect over another. Others, including a majority of the justices of the current Supreme Court, believe the term prohibits the government from promoting religion in general as well as the preference of one religion over another. In the words of the Court in *Everson*:

The establishment of religion clause means at least this: Neither a state nor the federal government may set up a church. Neither can pass laws that aid one religion, aid all religions, or prefer one religion over another. Neither can force a person to go to or to remain away from church against his will or force him to profess a belief or disbelief in any religion. . . . Neither a state or the federal government may, openly or secretly, participate in the affairs of any religious organizations or groups and vice versa. In the words of [Thomas] Jefferson, the clause against establishment of religion by law was intended to erect "a wall of separation between church and state."

To help interpret the establishment clause, the Court uses several tests, including the *Lemon*, coercion, endorsement and neutrality tests.

Tests Used to Interpret the Establishment Clause

Lemon *test*. The first of these tests is a three-part assessment sometimes referred to as the *Lemon* test. The test derives its name from the 1971 decision *Lemon v. Kurtzman*, in which the Court struck down a state program providing aid to religious elementary and secondary schools. Using the *Lemon* test, a court must first determine whether the law or government action in question has a bona fide secular purpose. This prong is based on the idea that government should only concern itself in civil matters, leaving religion to the conscience of the individual. Second, a court would ask whether the state action has the primary effect of advancing or inhibiting religion. Finally, the court would consider whether the action excessively entangles religion and government. While religion and government must interact at some points while co-existing in society, the concern here is that they do not so overlap and intertwine that people have difficulty differentiating between the two.

Although the test has come under fire from several Supreme Court justices, courts continue to use this test in most establishment-clause cases.

Lemon *test redux.* In its 1997 decision *Agostini v. Felton,* the Supreme Court modified the *Lemon* test. By combining the last two elements, the Court now used only the "purpose" prong and a modified version of the "effects" prong. The Court in *Agostini* identified three primary criteria for determining whether a government action has a primary effect of advancing religion: 1) government indoctrination, 2) defining the recipients of government benefits based on religion, and 3) excessive entanglement between government and religion.

Coercion test. Some justices propose allowing more government support for religion than the *Lemon* test allows. These justices support the adoption of a test outlined by Justice Anthony Kennedy in his dissent in *County of Allegheny v. ACLU* and known as the "coercion test." Under this test the government does not violate the establishment clause unless it (1) provides direct aid to religion in a way that would tend to establish a state church, or (2) coerces people to support or participate in religion against their will. Under such a test, the government would be permitted to erect such religious symbols as a Nativity scene standing alone in a public school or other public building at Christmas. But even the coercion test is subject to varying interpretations, as illustrated in *Lee v. Weisman,* the 1992 Rhode Island graduation-prayer decision in which Justices Kennedy and Antonin Scalia, applying the same test, reached different results.

Endorsement test. The endorsement test, proposed by Justice Sandra Day O'Connor, asks whether a particular government action amounts to an endorsement of religion. According to O'Connor, a government action is invalid if it creates a perception in the mind of a reasonable observer that the government is either endorsing or disapproving of religion. She expressed her understanding of the establishment clause in the 1984 case of *Lynch v. Donnelly,* in which she states, "The Establishment Clause prohibits government from making adherence to a religion relevant in any way to a person's standing in the political community." Her fundamental concern was whether the particular government action conveys "a message to non-adherents that they are outsiders, not full members of the political community, and an accompanying message to adherents that they are insiders, favored members of the political community." O'Connor's "endorsement test" has, on occasion, been subsumed into the *Lemon* test. The justices have simply incorporated it into the first two prongs of *Lemon* by asking if the challenged government act has the purpose or effect of advancing or endorsing religion.

The endorsement test is often invoked in situations where the government is engaged in expressive activities. Therefore, situations involving such things as graduation prayers, religious signs on government property, religion in the curriculum, etc., will usually be examined in light of this test.

Neutrality

While the Court looks to the endorsement test in matters of expression, questions involving use of government funds are increasingly determined under the rubric of neutrality. Under neutrality, the government would treat religious groups the same as other similarly situated groups. This treatment allows religious schools to participate in a generally available voucher program, allows states to provide computers to both religious and public schools, and allows states to provide reading teachers to low-performing students, even if they attend a religious school. . . . It also indicates that the faith-based initiatives proposed by President [George W.] Bush might be found constitutional, if structured appropriately.

The concept of neutrality in establishment-clause decisions evolved through the years. Cited first as a guiding principle in *Everson* neutrality meant government was neither ally nor adversary of religion. "Neutral aid" referred to the qualitative property of the aid, such as the funding going to the parent for a secular service such as busing. The rationale in *Everson* looked to the benefit to the parent, not to the religious school relieved of the responsibility of providing busing for its students.

Later cases recognized that all aid is in some way fungible, i.e. if a religious school receives free math texts from the state, then the money the school would have spent on secular texts can now be spent on religious material. This refocused the Court's attention not on the kind of aid that was provided, but who received and controlled the aid. Decisions involving vocational training scholarships and providing activity-fee monies to a college religious newspaper on the same basis as other student groups showed the Court focused on the individual's control over the funds and equal treatment between religious and non-religious groups.

In the 2002 case of *Zelman v. Simmons-Harris*, the plurality decision clearly defines neutrality as evenhandedness in terms of who may receive aid. A majority of the Court continues to find direct aid to religious institutions for use in religious activities unconstitutional, but indirect aid to a religious group appears constitutional, as long as it is part of a neutrally applied program that directs the money through a parent or other third party who ultimately controls the destination of the funds.

While many find this approach intuitively fair, others are dissatisfied. Various conservative religious groups raise concerns over diminishing the special place religion has historically played in constitutional law by treating religious freedom the same as every other kind of speech or discrimination claim. Strict separationist groups argue that providing government funds to religious groups violates the consciences of taxpayers whose faith may conflict with the religious missions of some groups who are eligible to receive funding using an "even-handed" approach.

Conclusion

Although the Court's interpretation of the establishment clause is in flux, it is likely that for the foreseeable future a majority of the justices will continue to view government neutrality toward religion as the guiding principle. Neutrality means not favoring one religion over another, not favoring religion over non-religion and vice versa.

Prayer in Public Schools Is Held to Be Unconstitutional

Hugo Black

In 1962 the U.S. Supreme Court ruled on the application of the establishment clause to prayer in public schools. In New Hyde Park, New York, the board of education had directed the school district's principal to have the following prayer said aloud in classrooms: "Almighty God, we acknowledge our dependence upon Thee, and we beg Thy blessings upon us, our parents, our teachers, and our country." The State Board of Regents, a group that had oversight over New York's public school system, had composed the prayer, which soon became the object of a lawsuit brought by the parents of ten pupils.

In a 6-1 decision known as *Engel v. Vitale,* the Supreme Court ruled that the prayer was unconstitutional as a violation of the establishment clause of the First Amendment. Justice Hugo Black delivered the opinion of the court. In the following excerpt he first gives the background to this case, noting the contents of the prayer and the resulting lawsuit. He then explains that the Court agrees with the petitioners that this prayer is unconstitutional because it was composed by government officials to promote religious beliefs. Black claims that even though the prayer is nondenominational and voluntary, it still involves indirect coercion because the government is behind it. Black was a Supreme Court associate justice from 1937 to 1971, where he was known as a defender of civil liberties. Prior to serving on the Court he was a lawyer and a U.S. senator.

T he respondent Board of Education of Union Free School District No. 9, New Hyde Park, New York, acting in its

Hugo Black, majority opinion, *Engel v. Vitale,* 1962.

official capacity under state law, directed the School District's principal to cause the following prayer to be said aloud by each class in the presence of a teacher at the beginning of each school day:

> Almighty God, we acknowledge our dependence upon Thee, and we beg Thy blessings upon us, our parents, our teachers and our country.

This daily procedure was adopted on the recommendation of the State Board of Regents, a governmental agency created by the State Constitution to which the New York Legislature has granted broad supervisory, executive, and legislative powers over the State's public school system. These state officials composed the prayer which they recommended and published as a part of their "Statement on Moral and Spiritual Training in the Schools," saying: "We believe that this Statement will be subscribed to by all men and women of good will, and we call upon all of them to aid in giving life to our program."

How the Case Began

Shortly after the practice of reciting the Regents' prayer was adopted by the School District, the parents of ten pupils brought this action in a New York State Court insisting that use of this official prayer in the public schools was contrary to the beliefs, religions, or religious practices of both themselves and their children. Among other things, these parents challenged the constitutionality of both the state law authorizing the School District to direct the use of prayer in public schools and the School District's regulation ordering the recitation of this particular prayer on the ground that these actions of official governmental agencies violate that part of the First Amendment of the Federal Constitution which commands that "Congress shall make no law respecting an establishment of religion"—a command which was "made applicable to the State of New York by the Fourteenth Amendment of the said Constitution." The New York Court of Appeals, over the dissents of Judges Dye and Fuld, sustained an order of the lower state courts which had upheld the power of New York to use the Regents' prayer as a part of the daily procedures of its public schools so long as the schools did not compel any pupil to join in the prayer over his or his parents' objection. We granted certiorari to review this important decision involving rights protected by the First and Fourteenth Amendments.

The Court's Finding

We think that by using its public school system to encourage recitation of the Regents' prayer, the State of New York has adopted a practice wholly inconsistent with the Establishment Clause. There can, of course, be no doubt that New York's program of daily classroom invocation of God's blessings as prescribed in the Regents' prayer is a religious activity. It is a solemn avowal of divine faith and supplication for the blessings of the Almighty. The nature of such a prayer has always been religious, none of the respondents has denied this and the trial court expressly so found:

> The religious nature of prayer was recognized by Jefferson and has been concurred in by theological writers, the United States Supreme Court and State courts and administrative officials, including New York's Commissioner of Education. A committee of the New York Legislature has agreed. The Board of Regents as *amicus curiae*, the respondents and intervenors all concede the religious nature of prayer, but seek to distinguish this prayer because it is based on our spiritual heritage. . . .

The petitioners contend among other things that the state laws requiring or permitting use of the Regents' prayer must be struck down as a violation of the Establishment Clause because that prayer was composed by governmental officials as a part of a governmental program to further religious beliefs. For this reason, petitioners argue, the State's use of the Regents' prayer in its public school system breaches the constitutional wall of separation between Church and State. We agree with that contention since we think that the constitutional prohibition against laws respecting an establishment of religion must at least mean that in this country it is no part of the business of government to compose official prayers for any group of the American people to recite as a part of a religious program carried on by government.

It is a matter of history that this very practice of establishing governmentally composed prayers for religious services was one of the reasons which caused many of our early colonists to leave England and seek religious freedom in America. The Book of Common Prayer, which was created under governmental direction and which was approved by Acts of Parliament in 1548 and 1549, set out in minute detail the accepted form and content of prayer and other religious ceremonies to be used in the established, tax-supported Church of England. The controversies over the Book and what should be its content repeatedly threatened to disrupt the peace of that country as the accepted forms of prayer in the established church changed with the views of the particular ruler that happened to be in control at the time. Powerful groups representing some of the varying religious views of the people struggled among themselves to impress their particular views upon the Government and obtain amendments of the Book more suitable to their respective notions of how religious services should be conducted in order that the official religious establishment would advance their particular religious beliefs. Other groups, lacking the necessary political power to influence the Government on the matter, decided to leave England and its established church and seek freedom in America from England's governmentally ordained and supported religion.

It is an unfortunate fact of history that when some of the very groups which had most strenuously opposed the established Church of England found themselves sufficiently in control of colonial governments in this country to write their own prayers into law, they passed laws making their own religion the official religion of their respective colonies. Indeed, as late as the time of the Revolutionary War, there were established churches in at least eight of the thirteen former colonies and established religions in at least four of the other five. But the successful Revolution against English political domination was shortly followed by intense opposition to the practice of establishing religion by law. This opposition crystallized rapidly into an effective political force in Virginia where the minority religious groups such as Presbyterians, Lutherans, Quakers and Baptists had gained such strength that the adherents to the established Episcopal Church were actually a minority themselves. In 1785–1786, those opposed to the established Church, led by James Madison and Thomas Jefferson, who, though themselves not members of any of these dissenting religious groups, opposed all religious establishments by law on grounds of principle, obtained the enactment of the famous "Virginia Bill for Religious Liberty" by which all religious groups were placed on an equal footing so far as the State was concerned. Similar though less far-reaching legislation was being considered and passed in other States.

The Constitution

By the time of the adoption of the Constitution, our history shows that there was a widespread awareness among many Americans of the dangers of a union of Church and State. These people knew, some of them from bitter personal experience, that one of the greatest dangers to the freedom of the individual to worship in his own way lay in the Government's placing its official stamp of approval upon one particular kind of prayer or one particular form of religious services. They knew the anguish, hardship and bitter strife that could come when zealous religious groups struggled with one another to obtain the Government's stamp of approval from each King, Queen, or Protector that came to temporary power. The Constitution was intended to avert a part of this danger by leaving the government of this country in the hands of the people rather than in the hands of any monarch. But this safeguard was not enough. Our Founders were no more willing to let the content of their prayers and their privilege of praying whenever they pleased be influenced by the ballot box than they were to let these vital matters of personal conscience depend upon the succession of monarchs. The First Amendment was added to the Constitution to stand as a guarantee that neither the power nor the prestige of the Federal Government would be used to control, support or influence the kinds of prayer the American people can say— that the people's religions must not be subjected to the pressures of government for change each time a new political administration is elected to office. Under that Amendment's prohibition against governmental establishment of religion, as reinforced by the provisions of the Fourteenth Amendment, government in this country, be it state or federal, is without power to prescribe by law any particular form of prayer which is to be used as an official prayer in carrying on any program of governmentally sponsored religious activity.

Why the Prayer Is Unconstitutional

There can be no doubt that New York's state prayer program officially establishes the religious beliefs embodied in the Regents' prayer. The respondents' argument to the contrary, which is largely based upon the contention that the Regents' prayer is "non-denominational" and the fact that the program, as modified and approved by state courts, does not require all pupils to recite the prayer but permits those who wish to do so to remain silent or be excused from the room, ignores the essential nature of the program's constitutional defects. Neither the fact that the prayer may be denominationally neutral, nor the fact that its observance on the part of the students is voluntary can serve to free it from the limitations of the Establishment Clause, as it might from the Free Exercise Clause, of the First Amendment, both of which are operative against the States by virtue of the Fourteenth Amendment. Although these two clauses may in certain instances overlap, they forbid two quite different kinds of governmental encroachment upon religious freedom. The Establishment Clause, unlike the Free Exercise Clause, does not depend upon any showing of direct governmental compulsion and is violated by the enactment of laws which establish an official religion whether those laws operate directly to coerce nonobserving individuals or not. This is not to say, of course, that laws officially prescribing a particular form of religious worship do not involve coercion of such individuals. When the power, prestige and financial support of government is placed behind a particular religions belief, the indirect coercive pressure upon religious minorities to conform to the prevailing officially approved religion is plain. But the purposes underlying the Establishment Clause go much further than that. Its first and most immediate purpose rested on the belief that a union of government and religion tends to destroy government and to degrade religion. The history of governmentally established religion, both in England and in this country, showed that whenever government had allied itself with one particular form of religion, the inevitable result had been that it had incurred the hatred, disrespect and even contempt of those who held contrary beliefs. That same history showed that many people had lost their respect for any religion that had relied upon the support of government to spread its faith. The Establishment Clause thus stands as an expression of principle on the part of the Founders of our Constitution that religion is too personal, too sacred, too holy, to permit its "unhallowed perversion" by a civil magistrate. Another purpose of the Establishment Clause rested upon an awareness of the historical fact that governmentally established religions and religious persecutions go hand in hand. The Founders knew that only a few years after the Book of Common Prayer became the only accepted form of religious services in the established Church of England, an Act of Uniformity was passed to compel all Englishmen to attend those services and to make it a criminal offense to conduct or attend religious gatherings of any other kind—a law which was consistently flouted by dissenting religious groups in England and which contributed to widespread persecutions of people like John Bunyan who persisted in holding "unlawful [religious] meetings . . . to the great disturbance and distraction of the good subjects of this kingdom. . . ." And they knew that similar persecutions had received the sanction of law in several of the colonies in this country soon after the establishment of official religions in those colonies. It was in large part to get completely away from this sort of systematic religious persecution that the Founders brought into being our Nation, our Constitution, and our Bill of Rights with its prohibition against any governmental

establishment of religion. The New York laws officially prescribing the Regents' prayer are inconsistent with both the
purposes of the Establishment Clause and with the Establishment Clause itself.

A Defense of the Ruling

It has been argued that to apply the Constitution in such a
way as to prohibit state laws respecting an establishment of
religious services in public schools is to indicate a hostility
toward religion or toward prayer. Nothing, of course, could
be more wrong. The history of man is inseparable from the
history of religion. And perhaps it is not too much to say that
since the beginning of that history many people have devoutly believed that "More things are wrought by prayer
than this world dreams of." It was doubtless largely due to
men who believed this that there grew up a sentiment that
caused men to leave the cross-currents of officially established state religions and religious persecution in Europe and
come to this country filled with the hope that they could find
a place in which they could pray when they pleased to the
God of their faith in the language they chose. And there were
men of this same faith in the power of prayer who led the
fight for adoption of our Constitution and also for our Bill of
Rights with the very guarantees of religious freedom that
forbid the sort of governmental activity which New York has
attempted here. These men knew that the First Amendment,
which tried to put an end to governmental control of religion
and of prayer, was not written to destroy either. They knew
rather that it was written to quiet well-justified fears which
nearly all of them felt arising out of an awareness that governments of the past had shackled men's tongues to make
them speak only the religious thoughts that government
wanted them to speak and to pray only to the God that government wanted them to pray to. It is neither sacrilegious
nor antireligious to say that each separate government in
this country should stay out of the business of writing or
sanctioning official prayers and leave that purely religious
function to the people themselves and to those the people
chose to look to for religious guidance.

It is true that New York's establishment of its Regents' prayer as an officially approved religious doctrine of that State does not amount to a total establishment of one particular religious sect to the exclusion of all others—that, indeed, the governmental endorsement of that prayer seems relatively insignificant when compared to the governmental encroachments upon religion which were commonplace 200 years ago. To those who may subscribe to the view that because the Regents' official prayer is so brief and general there can be no danger to religious freedom in its governmental establishment, however, it may be appropriate to say in the words of James Madison, the author of the First Amendment:

> It is proper to take alarm at the first experiment on our liberties. . . . Who does not see that the same authority which can establish Christianity, in exclusion of all other Religions, may establish with the same ease any particular sect of Christians, in exclusion of all other Sects? That the same authority which can force a citizen to contribute three pence only of his property for the support of any one establishment, may force him to conform to any other establishment in all cases whatsoever?

The judgment of the Court of Appeals of New York is reversed and the cause remanded for further proceedings not inconsistent with this opinion.

The Supreme Court Strikes Down Bible Readings in Public Schools

Tom C. Clark

In the past, many public school districts across America required some portions of the Bible to be read aloud during the day. In *Abington Township v. Schempp* (1963), the Supreme Court examined laws in two states—Pennsylvania and Maryland—that required Bible readings in public schools and found them to be unconstitutional. In the majority opinion, excerpted here, Justice Tom C. Clark concludes that compulsory religious exercises in public schools are a direct violation of the establishment clause.

Clark was an associate justice of the Supreme Court from 1949 to 1967. Prior to serving on the Court, he was a U.S. attorney general.

O nce again we are called upon to consider the scope of the provision of the First Amendment to the United States Constitution which declares that "Congress shall make no law respecting an establishment of religion or prohibiting the free exercise thereof. . . ." These companion cases present the issues in the context of state action requiring that schools begin each day with readings from the Bible. While raising the basic questions under slightly different factual situations, the cases permit of joint treatment. In light of the history of the First Amendment and of our cases interpreting and applying its requirements, we hold that the practices at issue and the laws requiring them are unconstitutional under the Establishment Clause, as applied to the states through the Fourteenth Amendment.

Tom C. Clark, majority opinion, *Abington Township v. Schempp*, 1963.

The Facts in Each Case: No. 142. The Commonwealth of Pennsylvania by law, 24 Pa. Stat. §15–1516, as amended, Pub. Law 1928 (Supp. 1960) Dec. 17, 1959, requires that "at least ten verses from the Holy Bible shall be read, without comment, at the opening of each public school on each school day. Any child shall be excused from such Bible reading, or attending such Bible reading, upon the written request of his parent or guardian." The Schempp family, husband and wife and two of their three children, brought suit to enjoin enforcement of the statute, contending that their rights under the Fourteenth Amendment to the Constitution of the United States are, have been, and will continue to be violated unless this statute be declared unconstitutional as violative of these provisions of the First Amendment. They sought to enjoin the appellant school district, wherein the Schempp children attend school, and its officers and the Superintendent of Public Instruction of the Commonwealth from continuing to conduct such readings and recitation of the Lord's Prayer in the public schools of the district pursuant to the statute. A three-judge statutory District Court for the Eastern District of Pennsylvania held that the statute is violative of the Establishment Clause of the First Amendment as applied to the states by the Due Process Clause of the Fourteenth Amendment and directed that appropriate injunctive relief issue. . . .

The appellees Edward Lewis Schempp, his wife Sidney, and their children, Roger and Donna, are of the Unitarian faith and are members of the Unitarian Church in Germantown, Philadelphia, Pennsylvania, where they, as well as another son, Ellory, regularly attend religious services. The latter was originally a party, but having graduated from the school system *pendente lite*, was voluntarily dismissed from the action. The other children attend the Abington Senior High School, which is a public school operated by appellant district.

On each school day at the Abington Senior High School between 8:15 and 8:30 A.M., while the pupils are attending their home rooms or advisory sections, opening services are conducted pursuant to the statute. The exercises are broadcast into each room in the school building through an intercommunications system and are conducted under the supervision of a teacher by students attending the school's radio and television workshop. Selected students from this course gather each morning in the school's workshop studio for the exercises, which include readings by one of the students of 10 verses of the Holy Bible, broadcast to each room in the building. This is followed by the recitation of the Lord's Prayer, likewise over the intercommunications system, but also by the students in the various classrooms, who are asked to stand and join in repeating the prayer in unison. The exercises are closed with the flag salute and such pertinent announcements as are of interest to the students. Participation in the opening exercises, as directed by the statute, is voluntary. The student reading the verses from the Bible may select the passages and read from any version he chooses, although the only copies furnished by the school are the King James version, copies of which were circulated to each teacher by the school district. During the period in which the exercises have been conducted the King James, the Douay and the Revised Standard versions of the Bible have been used, as well as the Jewish Holy Scriptures. There are no prefatory statements, no questions asked or solicited, no comments or explanations made and no interpretations given at or during the exercises. The students and parents are advised that the student may absent himself from the classroom or, should he elect to remain, not participate in the exercises.

It appears from the record that in schools not having an intercommunications system the Bible reading and the recitation of the Lord's Prayer were conducted by the homeroom teacher, who chose the text of the verses and read them herself or had students read them in rotation or by volunteers. This was followed by a standing recitation of the Lord's Prayer, together with the Pledge of Allegiance to the flag by the class in unison and a closing announcement of routine school items of interest.

The First Trial

At the first trial Edward Schempp and the children testified as to specific religious doctrines purveyed by a literal reading of the Bible "which were contrary to the religious beliefs they held and to their familial teaching." . . . The children testified that all of the doctrines to which they referred were read to them at various times as part of the exercises. Edward Schempp testified at the second trial that he had considered having Roger and Donna excused from attendance at the exercises but decided against it for several reasons, including his belief that the children's relationships with their teachers and classmates would be adversely affected. . . .

The trial court, in striking down the practices and the statute requiring them, made specific findings of fact that the children's attendance at Abington Senior High School is compulsory and that the practice of reading 10 verses from the Bible is also compelled by law. It also found that

> The reading of the verses, even without comment, possesses a devotional and religious character and constitutes in effect a religious observance. The devotional and religious nature of the morning exercises is made all the more apparent by the fact that the Bible reading is followed immediately by a recital in unison by the pupils of the Lord's Prayer. The fact that some pupils, or theoretically all pupils, might be excused from attendance at the exercises does not mitigate the obligatory nature of the ceremony for . . . Section 1516 . . . unequivocally requires the exercises to be held every school day in every school in the Commonwealth. The exercises are held in the school buildings and perforce are conducted by and under the authority of the local school authorities and during school sessions. Since the statute requires the reading of the "Holy Bible," a Christian document, the practice . . . prefers the Christian religion. The record demonstrates that it was the intention of . . . the Commonwealth . . . to introduce a religious ceremony into the public schools of the Commonwealth. . . .

Challenging the Law in Maryland

No. 119. In 1905 the Board of School Commissioners of Baltimore City adopted a rule pursuant to Art. 77, §202 of the

Annotated Code of Maryland. The rule provided for the holding of opening exercises in the schools of the city consisting primarily of the "reading, without comment, of a chapter in the Holy Bible and/or the use of the Lord's Prayer." The petitioners, Mrs. Madalyn Murray and her son, William J. Murray, III, are both professed atheists. Following unsuccessful attempts to have the respondent school board rescind the rule this suit was filed for mandamus to compel its rescission and cancellation. It was alleged that William was a student in a public school of the city and Mrs. Murray, his mother, was a taxpayer therein; that it was the practice under the rule to have a reading on each school morning from the King James version of the Bible; that at petitioners' insistence the rule was amended to permit children to be excused from the exercise on request of the parent and that William had been excused pursuant thereto; that nevertheless the rule as amended was in violation of the petitioners' rights "to freedom of religion under the First and Fourteenth Amendments" and in violation of "the principle of separation between church and state, contained therein. . . ." The petition particularized the petitioners' atheistic beliefs and stated that the rule, as practiced, violated their rights

> in that it threatens their religious liberty by placing a premium on belief as against non-belief and subjects their freedom of conscience to the rule of the majority; it pronounces belief in God as the source of all moral and spiritual values, equating these values with religious values, and thereby renders sinister, alien and suspect the belief and ideals of your Petitioners, promoting doubt and question of their morality, good citizenship and good faith.

The respondents demurred and the trial court, recognizing that the demurrer admitted all facts well pleaded, sustained it without leave to amend. The Maryland Court of Appeals affirmed, the majority of four justices holding the exercise not in violation of the First and Fourteenth Amendments, with three justices dissenting.

The American People and Religion

It is true that religion has been closely identified with our history and government. As we said in *Engel* v. *Vitale* (1962), "The history of man is inseparable from the history of religion. And . . . since the beginning of that history many people have devoutly believed that 'More things are wrought by prayer than this world dreams of.'" In *Zorach* v. *Clauson* (1952), we gave specific recognition to the proposition that "we are a religious people whose institutions presuppose a Supreme Being." The fact that the Founding Fathers believed devotedly that there was a God and that the unalienable rights of man were rooted in Him is clearly evidenced in their writings, from the Mayflower Compact to the Constitution itself. This background is evidenced today in our public life through the continuance in our oaths of office from the Presidency to the Alderman of the final supplication, "So help me God." Likewise each House of the Congress provides through its Chaplain an opening prayer, and the sessions of this Court are declared open by the crier in a short ceremony, the final phrase of which invokes the grace of God. Again, there are such manifestations in our military forces, where those of our citizens who are under the restrictions of military service wish to engage in voluntary worship. Indeed, only last year [1962] an official survey of the country indicated that 64% of our people have church membership, Bureau of Census, U.S. Department of Commerce, Statistical Abstract of the United States, . . . while less than 3% profess no religion whatever. . . . It can be truly said, therefore, that today, as in the beginning, our national life reflects a religious people who, in the words of [James] Madison, are "earnestly praying, as . . . in duty bound, that the Supreme Lawgiver of the Universe . . . guide them into every measure which may be worthy of his . . . blessing. . . ."

Almost a hundred years ago in *Minor* v. *Board of Education of Cincinnati*, Judge Alphonzo Taft, father of the revered Chief Justice, in an unpublished opinion stated the ideal of our people as to religious freedom as one of absolute equality before the law of all religious opinions and sects. . . .

The government is neutral, and, while protecting all, it prefers none, and it disparages none.

Before examining this "neutral" position in which the Establishment and Free Exercise Clauses of the First Amendment place our government it is well that we discuss the reach of the Amendment under the cases of this Court.

Past Cases

First, this Court has decisively settled that the First Amendment's mandate that "Congress shall make no law respecting an establishment of religion, or prohibiting the free exercise thereof has been made wholly applicable to the states by the Fourteenth Amendment. Twenty-three years ago in *Cantwell* v. *Connecticut* (1940), this Court, through Mr. Justice [Owen] Roberts, said:

> The fundamental concept of liberty embodied in that [Fourteenth] Amendment embraces the liberties guaranteed by the First Amendment. The First Amendment declares that Congress shall make no law respecting an establishment of religion or prohibiting the free exercise thereof. The Fourteenth Amendment has rendered the legislatures of the states as incompetent as Congress to enact such laws. . . .

In a series of cases since *Cantwell* the Court has repeatedly reaffirmed that doctrine, and we do so now. . . .

Second, this Court has rejected unequivocally the contention that the Establishment Clause forbids only governmental preference of one religion over another. Almost 20 years ago in *Everson*, the Court said that "neither a state nor the Federal government can set up a church. Neither can pass laws which aid one religion, aid all religions, or prefer one religion over another." . . . The same conclusion has been firmly maintained ever since that time . . . and we reaffirm it now.

While none of the parties to either of these cases has questioned these basic conclusions of the Court, both of which have been long established, recognized and consistently reaffirmed, others continue to question their history, logic and efficacy. Such contentions, in the light of the consistent interpretation in cases of this Court, seem entirely untenable and of value only as academic exercises.

The interrelationship of the Establishment and the Free Exercise Clauses was first touched upon by Mr. Justice Roberts for the Court in *Cantwell* v. *Connecticut*, where it was said that their "inhibition of legislation" had

> a double aspect. On the one hand, it forestalls compulsion by law of the acceptance of any creed or the practice of any form of worship. Freedom of conscience and freedom to adhere to such religious organization or form of worship as the individual may choose cannot be restricted by law. On the other hand, it safeguards the free exercise of the chosen form of religion. Thus the Amendment embraces two concepts—freedom to believe and freedom to act. The first is absolute but, in the nature of things, the second cannot be.

A half dozen years later in *Everson* v. *Board of Education*, this Court, through Mr. Justice [Hugo] Black, stated that the "scope of the First Amendment . . . was designed forever to suppress" the establishment of religion or the prohibition of the free exercise thereof. In short, the Court held that the Amendment

> requires the state to be a neutral in its relations with groups of religious believers and nonbelievers; it does not require the state to be their adversary. State power is no more to be used so as to handicap religions than it is to favor them. . . .

Finally, in *Engel* v. *Vitale*, [in 1962], these principles were so universally recognized that the Court without the citation of a single case and over the sole dissent of Mr. Justice [Potter] Stewart reaffirmed them. The Court found the 22-word prayer used in "New York's program of daily classroom invocation of God's blessings as prescribed in the Regents' prayer . . . [to be] a religious activity." It held that "it is no part of the business of government to compose official prayers for any group of the American people to recite as a part of a religious program carried on by the government." In discussing the reach of the Establishment and Free Exercise Clauses of the First Amendment the Court said:

> Although these two clauses may in certain instances overlap, they forbid two quite different kinds of governmental encroachment upon religious freedom. The Establishment Clause, unlike the Free Exercise Clause, does not depend upon any showing of direct governmental compulsion and is violated by the enactment of laws which establish an official religion whether those laws operate directly to coerce non-observing individuals or not. This is not to say, of course, that laws officially prescribing a particular form of religious worship do not involve coercion of such individuals. When the power, prestige and financial support of government is placed behind a particular religious belief, the indirect coercive pressure upon religious minorities to conform to the prevailing officially approved religion is plain.

And in further elaboration the Court found that the "first and most immediate purpose [of the Establishment Clause] rested on a belief that a union of government and religion tends to destroy government and to degrade religion." When government, the Court said, allies itself with one particular form of religion, the inevitable result is that it incurs "the hatred, disrespect, and even contempt of those who held contrary beliefs."

Government Neutrality

The wholesome "neutrality" of which this Court's cases speak thus stems from a recognition of the teachings of history that powerful sects or groups might bring about a fusion of governmental and religious functions or a concert or dependency of one upon the other to the end that official support of the State or Federal Government would be placed behind the tenets of one or of all orthodoxies. This the Establishment Clause prohibits. And a further reason for neutrality is found in the Free Exercise Clause, which recognizes the value of religious training, teaching and observance and, more particularly, the right of every person to freely choose his own course with reference thereto, free of any compulsion from the state. This the Free Exercise Clause guarantees. Thus, as we have seen, the two clauses may overlap. As we have indicated, the Establishment Clause has been directly considered by this Court eight times in the past score of years and, with only one Justice dissenting on the point, it has consistently held that the clause withdrew all legislative power respecting religious belief or the expression thereof. The test may be stated as follows: what are the purpose and the primary effect of the enactment? If either is the advancement or inhibition of religion then the enactment exceeds the scope of legislative power as circumscribed by the Constitution. That is to say that to withstand the strictures of the Establishment Clause there must be a secular legislative purpose and a primary effect that neither advances nor inhibits religion. . . . The Free Exercise Clause, likewise considered many times here, withdraws from legislative power, state and federal, the exertion of any restraint on the free exercise of religion. Its purpose is to secure religious liberty in the individual by prohibiting any invasions thereof by civil authority. Hence it is necessary in a free exercise case for one to show the coercive effect of the enactment as it operates against him in the practice of his religion. The distinction between the two clauses is apparent—a violation of the Free Exercise Clause is predicated on coercion while the Establishment Clause violation need not be so attended.

Application to This Case

Applying the Establishment Clause principles to the cases at bar we find that the States are requiring the selection and reading at the opening of the school day of verses from the Holy Bible and the recitation of the Lord's Prayer by the students in unison. These exercises are prescribed as part of the curricular activities of students who are required by law to attend school. They are held in the school buildings under the supervision and with the participation of teachers employed in those schools. None of these factors, other than compulsory school attendance, was present in the program upheld in *Zorach* v. *Clauson*. The trial court in No. 142 has found that such an opening exercise is a religious ceremony and was intended by the State to be so. We agree with the trial court's finding as to the religious character of the exercises. Given that finding the exercises and the law requiring them are in violation of the Establishment Clause.

There is no such specific finding as to the religious character of the exercises in No. 119, and the State contends (as does the State in No. 142) that the program is an effort to extend its benefits to all public school children without regard to their religious belief. Included within its secular purposes, it says, are the promotion of moral values, the contradiction to the materialistic trends of our times, the perpetuation of our institutions and the teaching of literature. The case came up on demurrer, of course, to a petition which alleged that the uniform practice under the rule had been to read from the King James version of the Bible and that the exercise was sectarian. The short answer, therefore, is that the religious character of the exercise was admitted by the State. But even if its purpose is not strictly religious, it is sought to be accomplished through readings, without comment, from the Bible. Surely the place of the Bible as an instrument of religion cannot be gainsaid, and the State's recognition of the pervading religious character of the ceremony is evident from the rule's specific permission of the alternative use of the Catholic Douay version as well as the recent amendment permitting non-attendance at the exercises. None of these factors is consistent with the contention that the Bible is here used either as an instrument for nonreligious moral inspiration or as a reference for the teaching of secular subjects.

The conclusion follows that in both cases the laws require religious exercises and such exercises are being conducted in direct violation of the rights of the appellees and petitioners. Nor are these required exercises mitigated by the fact that individual students may absent themselves upon parental request, for that fact furnishes no defense to a claim of unconstitutionality under the Establishment Clause. . . . Further, it is no defense to urge that the religious practices here may be relatively minor encroachments on the First Amendment. The breach of neutrality that is today a trickling stream may all too soon become a raging torrent and, in the words of Madison, "it is proper to take alarm at the first experiment on our liberties." . . .

It is insisted that unless these religious exercises are permitted a "religion of secularism" is established in the schools. . . . We do not agree, however, that this decision in any sense has that effect. In addition, it might well be said that one's education is not complete without a study of comparative religion or the history of religion and its relationship to the advancement of civilization. It certainly may be said that the Bible is worthy of study for its literary and historic qualities. Nothing we have said here indicates that such study of the Bible or of religion, when presented objectively as part of a secular program of education may not be effected consistent with the First Amendment. But the exercises here do not fall into those categories. They are religious exercises, required by the States in violation of the command of the First Amendment that the Government maintain strict neutrality, neither aiding nor opposing religion.

Finally, we cannot accept that the concept of neutrality, which does not permit a State to require a religious exercise even with the consent of the majority of those affected, collides with the majority's right to free exercise of religion. While the Free Exercise Clause clearly prohibits the use of state action to deny the right of free exercise to *anyone*, it has never meant that a majority could use the machinery of the State to practice its beliefs. . . .

The place of religion in our society is an exalted one, achieved through a long tradition of reliance on the home, the church and the inviolable citadel of the individual heart and mind. We have come to recognize through bitter experience that it is not within the power of government to invade that citadel, whether its purpose or effect be to aid or oppose, to advance or retard. In the relationship between man and religion, the State is firmly committed to a position of neutrality. Though the application of that rule requires interpretation of a delicate sort, the rule itself is clearly and concisely stated in the words of the First Amendment. Applying that rule to the facts of these cases, we affirm the judgment in No. 142. In No. 119, the judgment is reversed and the cause remanded to the Maryland Court of Appeals for further proceedings consistent with this opinion.

It is so ordered.

The Supreme Court Was Wrong to Bar Religion from Public Schools

David Lowenthal

David Lowenthal, who has taught political science at Boston College since 1966 and has served on the National Council for the Humanities, argues here that the Supreme Court was incorrect when it tossed out prayer and Bible readings from public schools. He says that Americans draw much of their morality from Judeo-Christian beliefs and that the best way to inculcate morality is to use the Bible and references to the belief in God. Lowenthal concludes that the Founders did not intend to bar religion from the schools. By interpreting the Constitution to do so, the Supreme Court has provoked hostility among much of the population.

In no area has the erroneous decision of the Court to apply the establishment clause against the states had graver implications than in public education. It should be clear to us, as it was to those founders of American public education, [Thomas] Jefferson and Horace Mann, that public schools have no more important function that the making of good citizens, men and women with the moral and intellectual attributes necessary to preserve democracy. This public function can involve a range of activities, including the teaching of rights and duties, the study of the deeds and discourses of our great men, and the practice of civic virtues inside and outside the schools. It requires inculcating the principles of the Declaration of Independence, but strongly emphasizing the duties corollary to rights that the Declaration implies but does not spell out, and admonishing the young to revere the Constitution and laws. It requires conveying some sense of the great challenges of republican self-government and instilling the moral qualities needed for the citizen to take care of himself, work well with others, and love his country: sturdy independence, sobriety, decency, neighborliness, patriotic concern for the common good.

The Value of God in Public Schools

Among a people drawing much of its morality from the Bible, such civic training cannot be accomplished without referring all to a just God and strengthening rational elements from the Declaration with religious elements from the Bible. When Jefferson designed a system of public education for Virginia, he spoke of using nonsectarian prayers drawn from the Bible, teaching the Declaration and the principles of natural theology and ethics, and even encouraging sectarian education and worship. In doing so, he laid down the main lines of what the states can constitutionally and prudentially do in their own interest. In his view, such practices did not violate the ban on religious establishments and the guarantee of free exercise found in Virginia's own constitution (since added in all other state constitutions). And they certainly do not violate any historically accurate reading of First Amendment liberties into the Fourteenth—supposing such reading necessary.[1]

In [*Abington Township v.*] *Schempp* [1963], where the Court struck down as an establishment of religion the use of Bible readings and the Lord's Prayer in the public schools, Justice [William] Brennan claimed the practice involved using "religious means to serve secular ends where secular means would suffice." He suggested that such important secular purposes as "fostering harmony and tolerance among the pupils, enhancing the authority of the teacher, and inspiring better discipline" may be served by various secular devices rather than by religion. But these purposes, mainly

1. refers to the Supreme Court's practice of interpreting the Fourteenth Amendment to mean that state laws must not violate the federal Constitution

dealing with conditions that should prevail within the schools, fall far short of what the states intended to accomplish with the help of Bible reading, which was the general training of citizens. And there is good reason to believe that public morality, in a country nourished on the Bible, is best taught by linking its principles to the belief in God. Certainly, a connection Jefferson, [George] Washington, [French statesman and author Alexis de] Tocqueville, and Mann all favored should not be subjected to airy dismissal by the Supreme Court, but left to reasonable legislative discretion.

The First Amendment, like its counterparts in state constitutions, forbids establishing any religion but does not forbid teaching the Declaration's teaching about "nature's God" and the rights and duties He supports. Nor does it forbid gathering from the Bible or the holy books of other Americans those passages that would reinforce the moral qualities needed for citizenship in American democracy. In Christian churches the Bible, used for its own sake, can be taken full strength and in all its parts and dimensions, but its place in the public schools is wholly and simply to serve the secular purposes for which the public schools exist. This requires a principled selectivity in finding passages that have the desired effect while avoiding passages that do not, whether because their moral point is unsuitable or their spirit sectarian. No doubt state legislatures or school boards should make clear their secular intent, and assure believing citizens that, in principle, all holy writings may contribute to this common civic purpose. The result will be not only to instill or reinforce the moral qualities citizens need, but to impress Americans with the degree to which the various religions agree on certain moral fundamentals and contribute to the well-being of American society. In short, the public employment of religion will help religion as well as civil society, guaranteeing it a lofty public place in the body politic.

While parts of the Bible and other scriptures may be helpful to American democracy, the backbone of American political belief clearly derives from reason rather than revelation, and displays itself for all to see in the Declaration of Independence. What the Declaration conveys, strictly speaking, is not a religion at all, but a set of beliefs, anchored in the existence of God, the Creator of the natural world. It calls for no common worship, no rituals, no priesthood; it has nothing to say about the various experiences of bliss or woe, from cradle to grave, around which religions build their most impressive ceremonies; it does not instruct us how to pursue happiness but concerns itself solely with the preservation of our rights. Thus, the public schools can and should teach the Declaration's rational core, supplemented by a stress on civic duties that are also known through reason to be such, but are better illustrated and more strikingly enjoined by various religions than by the Declaration itself. States that convey such necessary beliefs through their public schools, even with prayers, found or devised, which testify to them, are hardly establishing a religion; they are neither preferring one of the existing religions, nor creating a new one. What they are doing, or should be doing, is teaching the civic morality without which their form of government cannot endure.

Why the *Engel* Ruling Was Wrong

Before it was struck down as an establishment of religion in *Engel* [*v. Vitale* (1962)], the following prayer, composed by the State Board of Regents, was recited in New York's public schools: "Almighty God, we acknowledge our dependence upon Thee, and we beg Thy blessings upon us, our parents, our teachers and our country." The Regents had taken pains to write a nonsectarian prayer to which all believers could conscientiously subscribe, and had even gone so far as to allow students who could not—on whatever ground, religious or irreligious—to abstain from the proceeding. It was part of what they called "Moral and Spiritual Training in the Schools." The Court, through Justice [Hugo] Black, argued that prayer was a religious activity, and an official prayer the beginning of a religious establishment. Quoting copiously from [James] Madison's Memorial and Remonstrance, as if the First Amendment were simply an excerpt from that document, Black conjured up all the dangers of sectarian faction that the framers sought to prevent. A footnote toward the end of the opinion, we should recall, maintains that the Declaration's references to the Deity should not keep it from being recited as an historical document, and that school children can also be asked to sing official anthems (such as the "Star-Spangled Banner") which include "the composer's professions of faith in a Supreme Being."

There are several errors in Black's reasoning. The first is his failure to recognize that some references to God derive from philosophy and not from religion—as in the Declaration itself—and that therefore some form of prayer, directed at such a God, may conform to philosophy rather than religion. Consider the Declaration's references to "nature's God," to the "Creator," to the "Supreme Judge of the world," and to the "Protection of Divine Providence": would prayer to such a Being be inappropriate? Black's second error is to assume that a religious activity—supposing prayer to be such—implies a particular religion of which it is an activity. The Board of Regents tried to formulate, for school use, a prayer religious believers could agree upon generally. Thus, having school children express this prayer is not to form a new religion, but to ask them to avow for public purposes, in the classroom together, part of what they would express separately within their own churches and temples, or in the home. Precisely the same is true of the prayers opening daily sessions of Congress and the state legislatures, as well as the countless invocations of God's help and blessing found in presidential addresses. (Justice [Potter] Stewart, in his lone dissent, quotes such passages from Washington, Adams, Jefferson, Madison, Lincoln, Cleveland, Wilson, Roosevelt, Eisenhower, and Kennedy.) Even supposing these to be rooted in religious rather than philosophical beliefs, they certainly form no part of a particular organized religion, do not prefer one religion over another, and hence fail to constitute an establishment of religion. Or are presidents employing such invocations in their official utterances to be impeached for violating the Constitution?

The reasons which moved the Board of Regents to introduce such a prayer in the first place receive utterly no attention in the Court's opinion (or Justice [William] Douglas's concurrence). The Regents were not being frivolous or light-headed, though the wording of their prayer might well have been more copious and dignified, and better connected with historical precedent. They wanted students to sense a dependence on Almighty God, and to think of the benefits they should want to see brought not only to themselves but to parents, teachers, and country—that is, to those in whose debt they remain. They were intent on overcoming, in other words, the growing sense among the young that they are subject to no higher law, have no superior obligations, may act as they please, and think solely of themselves. In the name of civic education and morality, they were contradicting a dangerous egoism. Unfortunately, they were themselves contradicted by a Supreme Court that had nothing in its lexicon but the word "liberty," making it increasingly difficult for public authorities to inculcate that sense of duty and discipline without which liberty becomes a dangerous threat to others and oneself. Only recently, since the 1960s, has it become possible to call the public schools "godless" with any accuracy, a change concurrent with a precipitous decline in the teaching of citizenship and its demands, generally abetted by a Court that stripped school authorities of essential powers in order to magnify student rights. Thus has the Court contributed to the widespread spirit of laxity and lawlessness, aroused deep resentment within much of the population, and engendered a mounting conservative (and religious) reaction to its own "liberal" recasting of the Constitution.

Monotheism vs. Individual Rights

But the term "liberal" should not be conceded to those who are fanatics in the name of liberty, and who invoke the names of Madison and Jefferson without studying the fullness of their thought. These great men realized that the Declaration, anchored in monotheism, would itself anchor the American people's belief in inalienable rights, with the right of religious freedom included within the right to the pursuit of happiness. However paradoxical in appearance, the right to be different—in religion and other matters—depends for its effective continuance on the general public's not markedly differing about the right itself—that is, on a very widespread agreement concerning the right itself. The same is true of equality: no stronger basis can exist for the equal rights of all men, regardless of race, religion, sex, or ethnic background, than the teaching of the Declaration of Independence. To assure the most widespread conviction in connection with these rights, and at the same time in connection with the duties that alone can make the rights lastingly effective, is certainly a vital part of each state's authority, and the most important object of its educational system. This entails teaching the monotheism inherent in the Declaration, and against this imperious need no plea of individual rights should be permitted to prevail. Jefferson had no hesitation to require the study of the Declaration, as well as courses in natural theology and ethics, at the University of Virginia. Nothing in the First or Fourteenth Amendments keeps us from doing something similar today.

CHAPTER THREE

The Free-Exercise Clause and the Supreme Court

The Bill of Rights

Interpreting the Free-Exercise Clause: An Overview

Claire Mullally

Claire Mullally practiced law in New York City and Nashville, specializing in intellectual property law. She is now in the legal research department at the First Amendment Center, where she has studied and reported on the legal and cultural history of film censorship in the United States.

In the following article Mullally discusses the second of the two clauses in the First Amendment dealing with religious liberties—the free-exercise clause. She points out that conflict arises regarding this clause when laws that are religiously neutral have the unintended effect of interfering with religious practices. She then traces the history of free-exercise court cases that have attempted to address this issue. The first clash between state and church was *Reynolds v. United States* (1878), in which the Court decided that state concerns took precedence over Mormon religious practices. After the *Cantwell v. Connecticut* (1940) decision ruled that the free-exercise clause is applicable to the states, many more cases came to the Supreme Court. In *Sherbert v. Verner* (1963), the Court adopted the "compelling interest" standard, which holds that the government must have a compelling interest, such as national security, in order to limit someone's religious practices. One other case, *Wisconsin v. Yoder* (1972), reaffirmed the earlier *Sherbert* decision and held that a law that appears neutral to religion may actually violate the First Amendment if it burdens a religious practice.

Mullally says there was a revolution in free-exercise cases in the 1990 *Employment Division v. Smith* decision. The Court softened its stand toward government, allowing it to

Claire Mullally, "Free-Exercise Clause," www.firstamendmentcenter.org, July 5, 2003.

refuse to give people exemptions to laws that unintentionally hamper religion. This was a controversial decision because it abandoned the "compelling interest" standard. Since then, more than fifty free-exercise cases have been decided against religious groups and individuals. The Religious Freedom Restoration Act (RFRA), an attempt to reestablish the "compelling interest" standard, was passed by Congress but was struck down by the Supreme Court as it applied to state and local governments. Several states have passed their own RFRAs, but the level of protection under the free-exercise clause remains uncertain.

The free-exercise clause pertains to the right to freely exercise one's religion. It states that the government shall make no law prohibiting the free exercise of religion.

Although the text is absolute, the courts place some limits on the exercise of religion. For example, courts would not hold that the First Amendment protects human sacrifice even if some religion required it. The Supreme Court has interpreted this clause so that the freedom to believe is absolute, but the ability to act on those beliefs is not.

Questions of free exercise usually arise when a citizen's civic obligation to comply with a law conflicts with that citizen's religious beliefs or practices. If a law specifically singled out a specific religion or particular religious practice, under current Supreme Court rulings it would violate the First Amendment. Controversy arises when a law is generally applicable and religiously neutral but nevertheless has the "accidental" or "unintentional" effect of interfering with a particular religious practice or belief.

The Supreme Court has been closely divided on this issue. In its 1990 decision *Employment Division v. Smith*, the Court greatly narrowed a 35-year-old constitutional doctrine that had required a government entity to prove that it had a "compelling interest" whenever a generally applicable law was found to infringe on a claimant's religious beliefs or practices. Under current constitutional law as explained in *Smith*, a government burden on a religious belief or practice requires little justification as long as the law in question is determined to be generally applicable and does not target a specific religion or religious practice. The Court in 1993 clarified how these principles were to apply in *Church of the Lukumi Babalu Aye v. City of Hialeah*. There, the Court closely analyzed a facially neutral and generally applicable law and determined that it was neither neutral nor generally applicable. Since the law burdened a religious practice (here the animal sacrifice ritual of the Santeria religion), the government would have to demonstrate that it had a compelling interest in passing the law. The Court would then "strictly scrutinize" the government's claims. In *Hialeah*, the government could not meet this burden and the law was struck down.

Early Court Decisions

The first Supreme Court case that addressed the issue of free exercise was *Reynolds v. U.S.* (1878), in which the Court upheld a federal law banning polygamy over objections by Mormons who claimed that the practice was their religious duty. The Court in *Reynolds* distinguished between religious belief and religious conduct or action, stating that Congress was "deprived of all legislative power over mere opinion, but was left free to reach actions which were in violation of social duties or subversive to good order." Recognizing the religious defense, the Court said, would "permit every citizen to become a law unto himself." While the government could not punish citizens because of their religious beliefs, it could regulate religiously motivated conduct, provided that it had a rational basis for doing so. This "rational basis test" became the standard for determining whether a law that impinged on a religious practice violated the free-exercise clause. As that standard was easy for the government to satisfy, for almost a century the courts generally rejected religious-freedom claims against generally applicable laws.

It is important to note also that until the decision of *Cantwell v. Connecticut* (1940), opened the door to federal litigation against the states for religion-clause claims (by ruling that the 14th Amendment's protections against state action "incorporates" or absorbs, the free-exercise clause of the First Amendment) there was no cause of action against the state for laws that may have impinged on religious practices. In effect, the Supreme Court did not have opportunity to review this issue until the mid-20th century, when various free-exercise clause cases made their way through the state courts to the Supreme Court.

In its 1963 decision *Sherbert v. Verner*, the Supreme Court found that the Constitution afforded at least some degree of government accommodation of religious practices. Adele Sherbert, a Seventh-day Adventist, was discharged by her South Carolina employer because she would not work on Saturday, her faith's Sabbath. When she could not find other employment that would not require her to work on Saturday, she filed a claim for unemployment benefits. South Carolina law provided that a person was ineligible for benefits if he or she failed, without good cause, to accept available suitable employment when offered. The state denied Sherbert benefits, saying she had not accepted suitable employment when offered, even though she was required to work on her Sabbath. The decision was upheld by the South Carolina Supreme Court.

The U.S. Supreme Court reversed the state court decision. Justice William Brennan wrote that although the Court had theretofore "rejected challenges under the Free Exercise Clause to governmental regulation of certain overt acts prompted by religious beliefs and principles," the conduct or actions so regulated had "invariably posed some substantial threat to public safety, peace or order." Since Sherbert's "conscientious objection to Saturday work" was not "conduct within the reach of state legislation," any law that resulted in an incidental burden to the free exercise of her religion must be justified by a "compelling state interest in the regulation of a subject within the State's power to regulate."

Thus, in *Sherbert*, the Court adopted a "compelling interest" standard that government must meet when a generally applicable law unintentionally burdened a claimant's religious practices and beliefs. The state in *Sherbert* could not demonstrate such compelling interest: the mere possibility that allowing exemptions to the unemployment compensation laws for Saturday worshipers might result in fraudulent or spurious claims was not sufficiently compelling, the Court reasoned. Even if an increase in fraudulent claims could be proved, the state would nevertheless have to show that no alternative regulations could "combat such abuses without infringing First Amendment rights," thus also introducing a doctrine requiring the government to demonstrate that it used the "least restrictive" means when enacting legislation that burdened a religious belief or practice.

It is interesting and important to note the legal and social context in which Justice Brennan articulated this "compelling state interest" standard for free-exercise clause claims. The civil rights litigation of the 1950s and 1960s had greatly informed the Court's perspective. It had become clear to Brennan that the Court must give a "heightened scrutiny" to cases in which fundamental rights were at stake and require the state to demonstrate that the law in question served only interests that were of paramount importance. A law having a merely "rational," "important," "valid" or "legitimate" purpose could not withstand a claim that it infringed on a fundamental right.

In 1972, the Court reaffirmed that a generally applicable law, "neutral on its face" may nonetheless violate the First Amendment if such law "unduly burdens the practice of religion." In *Wisconsin v. Yoder*, the Court held that the state's interest in requiring a child's compulsory attendance at school through age 16, though important, could not withstand a free-exercise claim by members of the Amish religious sect. An Amish family claimed that requiring their children to attend public schools after age 14 would expose them to "wordly influences" against their traditionalist beliefs and undermine the insular Amish community. The Court in *Yoder* noted that the purpose of mandatory education was to develop a productive, self-reliant citizenry, but that the state's purpose must be examined in light of the particular circumstances of the case. Since the Amish had a 200-year tradition of training their adolescents to be productive members of their "separated agrarian" community, the government's interests could still be achieved by requiring education only through age 14.

This would obviate the burden to the Amish community's right to freely exercise its religion, while the state's overriding interest would still be served. In a clear statement of its doctrine, the Court in *Yoder* held that "[o]nly those interests of the highest order and those not otherwise served can overbalance legitimate claims to the free exercise of religion."

After *Sherbert* and *Yoder*, the Court applied the religious-exemption doctrine by examining two questions: Has the government significantly burdened a sincerely motivated religious practice? If so, is the burden justified by a compelling state interest? Increasingly, however, the Court narrowed the concept of a "significant burden" to religion and in a series of decisions throughout the 1980s, the Court rejected many free-exercise claims on this basis. The Court also became more willing to label state interests as "compelling" in cases where religious practice was significantly burdened by a general law.

A Huge Change in Court Rulings

It was clear that the Supreme Court was struggling with the issue of requiring accommodations based on the compelling-interest standard. In its 1990 decision *Employment Division v. Smith*, still a highly controversial opinion, the Court ruled that it would no longer give heightened scrutiny to the government's refusal to grant exemptions to generally applicable laws that unintentionally burden religious beliefs or practices.

In *Smith*, two counselors were fired from their jobs with a private drug rehabilitation organization because they ingested peyote at a ceremony of the Native American Church. The two men, members of the Native American Church, were determined to be ineligible for unemployment benefits because they had been fired for work-related "misconduct." The Oregon Supreme Court held that the prohibition against sacramental peyote use was invalid under the free-exercise clause and thus the men could not be denied unemployment benefits for such use. The U.S. Supreme Court held that the free-exercise clause permits the state to prohibit sacramental peyote use and the state can thus deny unemployment benefits to persons discharged for such use.

Justice Antonin Scalia, writing for the majority, declined to apply the balancing test of *Sherbert v. Verner*, greatly limiting the scope of that precedent. Instead Scalia reached back to the early opinion in *Reynolds v. U.S.* (the polygamy case), claiming that to require the government to show a "compelling interest" in enforcing a generally applicable law when such a law impedes on religiously motivated conduct permits the individual "to become a law unto himself," "invites anarchy" and would produce a "constitutional anomaly." It would, Scalia claimed, make a citizen's obligation to obey the law contingent on his religious beliefs. Scalia found that the Court had never in fact invalidated any government action on the basis of the *Sherbert* compelling-interest test except the denial of unemployment compensation (that *Smith* was itself an unemployment compensation case is not addressed in the decision). Scalia further stated that the only decisions in which the Court had held that the First Amendment barred the application of a generally applicable law to religiously motivated conduct involved not just free-exercise clause claims, but those claims *in conjunction with* other constitutional protections, such as freedom of speech and the press or the right of parents to direct the education of their children (*Yoder*). The *Smith* case, the Court said, did not involve such a "hybrid situation."

Justice Sandra Day O'Connor, although concurring in the outcome, vigorously disagreed with the Court's abandonment of the "compelling interest" standard, as did Justice Harry Blackmun in the dissent. O'Connor reasoned that the free-exercise clause provides relief from a burden imposed by government whether the burden is imposed directly through laws that prohibit specific religious practices, which would be clearly unconstitutional, or indirectly through laws that "in effect make abandonment of one's own religion . . . the price of an equal place in society."

Recent Free-Exercise Cases

In the three years following *Smith*, more than 50 reported free-exercise cases were decided against religious groups and individuals. As a result, more than 60 religious and civil liberties groups, including the American Civil Liberties Union,

Concerned Women for America, People for the American Way and the National Association of Evangelicals, joined to draft and support the passage of the Religious Freedom Restoration Act—or RFRA. The act, which was signed by President [Bill] Clinton on Nov. 17, 1993, restored the compelling-interest test and ensured its application in all cases where religious exercise is substantially burdened.

Also in 1993, the Supreme Court re-visited the religious exemption issue in *City of Hialeah*. After a Santeria church announced plans to establish a house of worship in Hialeah [Florida], the city enacted an ordinance prohibiting the ritual slaughter or sacrifice of animals, which is one of the religion's principal forms of devotion. The Supreme Court found that the history of the ordinance showed that it specifically targeted the Santeria practice of animal sacrifice while providing numerous exemptions for other instances of animal slaughter, including Kosher slaughter. Since the ordinance both burdened religious practice and was neither neutral nor generally applicable, the Court would apply "strict scrutiny" and the "compelling interest" standard to the city's actions. The ordinances could not withstand such scrutiny, the Court stated, holding them invalid under the free-exercise clause.

After *City of Hialeah*, the inquiry into whether a law is in fact "neutral" and "generally applicable" has provided claimants with ammunition in free-exercise clause claims. . . . Many "general" laws provide categorical exceptions of one kind or another. Arguably, once a legislature has carved out an exemption for a secular group or person, the law is no longer "generally applicable," and thus subject to the *City of Hialeah* standard of strict scrutiny. Similarly, a claimant may prevail if he can prove that a law of general applicability that burdens religion is unevenly enforced. . . . However, some lower courts have interpreted *City of Hialeah* to mean that religious claimants must demonstrate an anti-religious motive when challenging a law that on its face is generally applicable, a difficult standard to prove.

While widely supported, RFRA was short-lived. On June 25, 1997, the Supreme Court, by a vote of 6-3, struck down the act as applied to state and local governments. The Court in *City of Boerne v. Flores* held that Congress overstepped its bounds by forcing states to provide more protection for religious liberty than the First Amendment, as interpreted by the Supreme Court in *Employment Division v. Smith*, required. While RFRA no longer applies to the states, it is still applicable to the federal government, as seen recently in several district court decisions.

In 2000, President Clinton signed the Religious Land Use and Institutionalized Persons Act, or RLUIPA, which mandates the use of the compelling-interest and least-restrictive means standards for free-exercise cases that involve infringements on religion from land-use laws and to persons institutionalized in prisons, hospitals and retirement or nursing homes. Cases challenging the constitutionality of RLUIPA are also making their way through the federal appellate courts. . . .

Eleven states have passed their own RFRAs, all of which reinstate the compelling-interest test to varying degrees. In other states—such as Minnesota, Massachusetts and Wisconsin—the courts have held that the compelling-interest test is applicable to religion claims by virtue of their own state constitutions. In many states, however, the level of protection that applies to free-exercise claims is uncertain.

The jurisprudence regarding religious exemptions to generally applicable laws is clearly still in flux, providing an uneven and uncertain patchwork of protections to religious adherents.

The Government May Restrict Religious Practice

Morrison R. Waite

Although the Constitution guarantees religious liberty, this freedom must be limited when religious practices clash with government laws. The first time such a clash ended up at the Supreme Court was in the 1878 *Reynolds v. United States* case. Congress had enacted a statute making polygamy a criminal offense when Utah, home to Mormons who believed polygamy was a religious duty, was still a territory. Reynolds was convicted for violating the law, but he argued he should be allowed to engage in polygamy because he was required to do so by his religious faith. He claimed that this law impaired his free exercise of religion. The decision, excerpted below from the majority opinion by Chief Justice Morrison R. Waite, ruled against Reynolds, making a distinction between religious faith and religious practice. People may believe anything they wish, but their activities can be regulated to restrain antisocial conduct. This decision became a leading case, often cited and quoted. Waite was the chief justice of the Supreme Court from 1874 to 1888.

This is an indictment for bigamy under Section 5352, Revised Statutes, which, omitting its exceptions, is as follows: "Every person having a husband or wife living, who marries another, whether married or single, in a Territory, or other place over which the United States have exclusive jurisdiction, is guilty of bigamy, and shall be punished by a fine of not more than $500, and by imprisonment for a term of not more than five years." . . .

Morrison R. Waite, majority opinion, *Reynolds v. United States,* 1878.

The Current Case

On the trial, the plaintiff in error, the accused, proved that at the time of his alleged second marriage he was, and for many years before had been, a member of the Church of Jesus Christ of Latter-Day Saints, commonly called the Mormon Church, and a believer in its doctrines; that it was an accepted doctrine of that church "That it was the duty of male members of said Church, circumstances permitting, to practice polygamy: . . . that this duty was enjoined by different books which the members of said Church believed to be of divine origin, and among others the Holy Bible, and also that the members of the Church believed that the practice of polygamy was directly enjoined upon the male members thereof by the Almighty God, in a revelation to Joseph Smith, the founder and prophet of said Church; that the failing or refusing to practice polygamy by such male members of said Church, when circumstances would admit, would be punished, and that the penalty for such failure and refusal would be damnation in the life to come." He also proved "That he had received permission from the recognized authorities in said Church to enter into polygamous marriage; . . . that Daniel H. Wells, one having authority in said Church to perform the marriage ceremony, married the said defendant on or about the time the crime is alleged to have been committed, to some woman by the name of Schofield, and that such marriage ceremony was performed under and pursuant to the doctrines of said Church."

Upon this proof he asked the court to instruct the jury that if they found from the evidence that he "was married as charged (if he was married) in pursuant of and in conformity with what he believed at the time to be religious duty, that the verdict must be 'not guilty.'" This request was refused, and the court did charge "That there must have been a criminal intent, but that if the defendant, under the influence of a religious belief that it was right—under an inspiration, if you please, that it was right—deliberately married a second time, having a first wife living, the want of consciousness of evil intent, the want of understanding on his part that he was committing a crime, did not excuse him; but the law inexorably in such case implies the criminal intent."

Upon this charge and refusal to charge the question is raised, whether religious belief can be accepted as a justification of an overt act made criminal by the law of the land. The inquiry is not as to the power of Congress to prescribe criminal laws for the Territories, but as to the guilt of one who knowingly violates a law which has been properly enacted, if he entertains a religious belief that the law is wrong.

Congress cannot pass a law for the government of the Territories which shall prohibit the free exercise of religion. The first amendment to the Constitution expressly forbids such legislation. Religious freedom is guaranteed everywhere throughout the United States, so far as congressional interference is concerned. The question to be determined is, whether the law now under consideration comes within this prohibition.

A Historical Look at Free Exercise

The word "religion" is not defined in the Constitution. We must go elsewhere, therefore, to ascertain its meaning, and nowhere more appropriately, we think, than to the history of the times in the midst of which the provision was adopted. The precise point of the inquiry is, what is the religious freedom which has been guaranteed?

Before the adoption of the Constitution, attempts were made in some of the Colonies and States to legislate not only in respect to the establishment of religion, but in respect to its doctrines and precepts as well. The people were taxed, against their will, for the support of religion, and sometimes for the support of particular sects to whose tenets they could not and did not subscribe. Punishments were prescribed for a failure to attend upon public worship, and sometimes for entertaining heretical opinions. The controversy upon this general subject was animated in many of the States, but seemed at last to culminate in Virginia. In 1784, the House of Delegates of that State having under consideration "A bill establishing provision for teachers of the Christian religion," postponed it until the next session, and directed that the bill should be published and distributed, and that the People be requested "to signify their opinion respecting the adoption of such a bill at the next session of Assembly."

This brought out a determined opposition. Amongst others, Mr. [James] Madison prepared a "Memorial and Remonstrance," which was widely circulated and signed, and in which he demonstrated "that religion, or the duty we owe the Creator," was not within the cognizance of civil government. At the next session the proposed bill was not only defeated, but another, "for establishing religious freedom," drafted by Mr. [Thomas] Jefferson, was passed. In the preamble of this Act religious freedom is defined; and after a recital "That to suffer the civil magistrate to intrude his powers into the field of opinion, and to restrain the profession or propagation of principles on supposition of their ill tendency, is a dangerous fallacy which at once destroys all religious liberty," it is declared "that it is time enough for the rightful purposes of civil government for its officers to interfere when principles break out into overt acts against peace and good order." In these two sentences is found the true distinction between what properly belongs to the Church and what to the State.

Building a Wall of Separation

In a little more than a year after the passage of this statute the convention met which prepared the Constitution of the United States. Of this convention Mr. Jefferson was not a member, he being then absent as minister to France. As soon as he saw the draft of the Constitution proposed for adoption, he, in a letter to a friend, expressed his disappointment at the absence of an express declaration insuring the freedom of religion, but was willing to accept it as it was, trusting that the good sense and honest intentions of the people would bring about the necessary alterations. Five of the States, while adopting the Constitution, proposed amendments. Three, New Hampshire, New York and Virginia, included in one form or another a declaration of religious freedom in the changes they desired to have made, as did also North Carolina, where the convention at first declined to ratify the Constitution until the proposed amendments were acted upon. Accordingly, at the first session of the first Congress the amendment now under consideration was proposed with others by Mr. Madison. It met the views of the advocates of religious freedom, and was adopted. Mr. Jefferson afterwards, in reply to an address to him by a committee of the Danbury Baptist Association, took occasion to say: "Believing with you that religion is a matter which lies solely between man and his God; that he owes account to none other for his faith or his worship; that the legislative powers of the Government reach actions only, and not opinions, I contemplate with sovereign reverence that act of the whole American people which declared that their Legislature should 'make no law respecting an establishment of religion or prohibiting the free exercise thereof,' thus building a wall of separation between Church and State. Adhering to this expression of the Supreme will of the Nation in behalf of the rights of conscience, I shall see, with sincere satisfaction, the progress of those sentiments which tend to restore man to all his natural rights, convinced he has no natural right in opposition to his social duties." Coming as this does from an acknowledged leader of the advocates of the measure, it may be accepted almost as an authoritative declaration of the scope and effect of the amendment thus secured. Congress was deprived of all legislative power over mere opinion, but was left free to reach actions which were in violation of social duties or subversive of good order.

Polygamy: An Offense Against Society

Polygamy has always been odious among the Northern and Western Nations of Europe and, until the establishment of the Mormon Church, was almost exclusively a feature of the life of Asiatic and African people. At common law, the second marriage was always void, and from the earliest history of England polygamy has been treated as an offense against society. After the establishment of the ecclesiastical courts, and until the time of James I, it was punished through the instrumentality of those tribunals, not merely because ecclesiastical rights had been violated, but because upon the separation of the ecclesiastical courts from the civil, the ecclesiastical were supposed to be the most appropriate for the trial of matrimonial causes and offenses against the rights of marriage; just as they were for testamentary causes and the settlement of the estates of deceased persons.

By the Statute of 1 James I, ch. 11, the offense, if committed in England or Wales, was made punishable in the civil courts, and the penalty was death. As this statute was limited in its operation to England and Wales, it was at a very early period re-enacted, generally with some modifications, in all the Colonies. In connection with the case we are now considering, it is a significant fact that on the 8th of December, 1788, after the passage of the Act establishing religious freedom, and after the convention of Virginia had recommended as an amendment to the Constitution of the United States the declaration in a Bill of Rights that "All men have an equal, natural and unalienable right to the free exercise of religion, according to the dictates of conscience," the Legislature of that State substantially enacted the Statute of James I, death penalty included, because as recited in the preamble, "It hath been doubted whether bigamy or polygamy be punishable by the laws of this Commonwealth." From that day to this we think it may safely be said there never has been a time in any State of the Union when polygamy has not been an offense against society, cognizable by the civil courts and punishable with more or less severity. In the face of all this evidence, it is impossible to believe that the constitutional guaranty of religious freedom was intended to prohibit legislation in respect to this most important feature of social life. Marriage, while from its very nature a sacred obligation, is, nevertheless, in most civilized nations, a civil contract, and usually regulated by law. . . . There cannot be a doubt that, unless restricted by some form of constitution, it is within the legitimate scope of the power of every civil government to determine whether polygamy or monogamy shall be the law of social life under its dominion.

A Crime Knowingly Committed

In our opinion the statute immediately under consideration is within the legislative power of Congress. It is constitutional and valid as prescribing a rule of action for all those residing in the Territories, and in places over which the United States have exclusive control. This being so, the only question which remains is, whether those who make polygamy a part of their religion are excepted from the operation of the statute. If they are, then those who do not make polygamy a part of their religious belief may be found guilty and punished, while those who do must be acquitted and go free. This would be introducing a new element into criminal law. Laws are made for the government of actions, and while they cannot interfere with mere religious belief and opinions, they may with practices. Suppose one believed that human sacrifices were a necessary part of religious worship, would it be seriously contended that the civil government under which he lived could not interfere to prevent a sacrifice? Or if a wife religiously believed it was her duty to burn herself upon the funeral pyre of her dead husband, would it be beyond the power of the civil government to prevent her carrying her belief into practice?

So here, as a law of the organization of society under the exclusive dominion of the United States, it is provided that plural marriages shall not be allowed. Can a man excuse his practices to the contrary because of his religious belief? To permit this would be to make the professed doctrines of religious belief superior to the law of the land, and in effect to permit every citizen to become a law unto himself. Government could exist only in name under such circumstances.

A criminal intent is generally an element of crime, but every man is presumed to intend the necessary and legitimate consequences of what he knowingly does. Here the accused knew he had once been married, and that his first wife was living. He also knew that his second marriage was forbidden by law. When, therefore, he married the second time, he is presumed to have intended to break the law. And the breaking of the law is the crime. Every act necessary to constitute the crime was knowingly done, and the crime was, therefore, knowingly committed. Ignorance of a fact may sometimes be taken as evidence of a want of criminal intent, but not ignorance of the law. The only defense of the accused in this case is his belief that the law ought not to have been enacted. It matters not that his belief was a part of his professed religion; it was still belief, and belief only.

In *Regina v. Wagstaffe*, the parents of a sick child, who omitted to call in medical attendance because of their religious belief that what they did for its cure would be effective, were held not to be guilty of manslaughter, while it was said the contrary would have been the result if the child had actually been starved to death by the parents, under the notion that it was their religious duty to abstain from giving it food. But when the offense consists of a positive act which is knowingly done, it would be dangerous to hold that the offender might escape punishment because he religiously believed the law which he had broken ought never to have been made. No case, we believe, can be found that has gone so far.

No Child May Be Coerced into Saying a Flag Pledge

Robert H. Jackson

In 1935 the religious group Jehovah's Witnesses declared flag salutes to be a violation of a biblical command against worshipping graven images. A few years later, in 1940, a case on this topic made its way to the U.S. Supreme Court. The judges decided in this case, *Minersville School District v. Gobitis*, that a Pennsylvania school district was correct when it expelled three Jehovah's Witnesses children who refused to salute the flag at a public school.

Just three years later the Court reversed itself in *West Virginia State Board of Education v. Barnette*. It ruled that the board of education's decision to expel students who refused to salute the flag violated the First Amendment. How did this turnaround happen so quickly? Two new members had recently joined the Court, and several of the older members admitted that the first decision was incorrect. In the opinion excerpted below, Justice Robert H. Jackson argues that the *Gobitis* case had been decided due to a need for national unity during wartime. He and the other concurring judges insist that national unity cannot be achieved by coercion. In fact, the Bill of Rights was set up in part to prevent government from controlling public opinion. The Constitution limits what government can declare as orthodox and what it can force people to agree to.

Jackson was an associate justice of the Supreme Court from 1941 to 1954. In 1945 and 1946 he served as U.S. chief counsel at the Nuremberg war crimes trials.

Robert H. Jackson, majority opinion, *West Virginia State Board of Education v. Barnette,* 1945.

The Board of Education on January 9, 1942, adopted a resolution containing recitals taken largely from the Court's *Gobitis* opinion and ordering that the salute to the flag become "a regular part of the program of activities in the public schools," that all teachers and pupils "shall be required to participate in the salute honoring the Nation represented by the Flag; provided, however, that refusal to salute the Flag be regarded as an Act of insubordination, and shall be dealt with accordingly." . . .

Failure to conform is "insubordination" dealt with by expulsion. Readmission is denied by statute until compliance. Meanwhile the expelled child is "unlawfully absent" and may be proceeded against as a delinquent. His parents or guardians are liable to prosecution, and if convicted are subject to fine not exceeding $50 and jail term not exceeding thirty days.

The Case Before the Court

Appellees, citizens of the United States and of West Virginia, brought suit in the United States District Court for themselves and others similarly situated asking its injunction to restrain enforcement of these laws and regulations against Jehovah's Witnesses. The Witnesses are an unincorporated body teaching that the obligation imposed by law of God is superior to that of laws enacted by temporal government. Their religious beliefs include a literal version of Exodus, Chapter 20, verses 4 and 5, which says: "Thou shalt not make unto thee any graven image, or any likeness of anything that is in heaven above, or that is in the earth beneath, or that is in the water under the earth; thou shalt not bow down thyself to them, nor serve them." They consider that the flag is an "image within this command." For this reason they refuse to salute it.

Children of this faith have been expelled from school and are threatened with exclusion for no other cause. Officials threaten to send them to reformatories maintained for criminally inclined juveniles. Parents of such children have been prosecuted and are threatened with prosecutions for causing delinquency. . . .

The case was submitted on the pleadings to a district Court of three judges. It restrained enforcement as to the plaintiffs and those of that class. The Board of Education brought the case here by direct appeal.

This case calls upon us to reconsider a precedent decision, as the Court throughout its history often has been required to do. Before turning to the *Gobitis* case, however, it is desirable to notice certain characteristics by which this controversy is distinguished.

The freedom asserted by these appellees does not bring them into collision with rights asserted by any other individual. It is such conflicts which most frequently require intervention of the State to determine where the rights of one end and those of another begin. . . . The sole conflict is between authority and rights of the individual. The State asserts power to condition access to public education on making a prescribed sign and profession and at the same time to coerce attendance by punishing both parent and child. The latter stand on a right of self-determination in matters that touch individual opinion and personal attitude. . . .

There is no doubt that, in connection with the pledges, the flag salute is a form of utterance. . . .

To sustain the compulsory flag salute we are required to say that a Bill of Rights which guards the individual's right to speak his own mind, left it open to public authorities to compel him to utter what is not in his mind. . . .

Nor does the issue as we see it turn on one's possession of particular religious views or the sincerity with which they are held. While religion supplies appellees' motive for enduring the discomforts of making the issue in this case, many citizens who do not share these religious views hold such a compulsory rite to infringe constitutional liberty of the individual. It is not necessary to inquire whether nonconformist beliefs will exempt from the duty to salute unless we first find power to make the salute a legal duty.

The *Gobitis* decision, however, *assumed*, as did the argument in that case and in this, that power exists in the State to impose the flag salute discipline upon school children in general. The Court only examined and rejected a claim based on religious beliefs of immunity from an unquestioned general rule. The question which underlies the flag salute controversy is whether such a ceremony so touching matters of opinion and political attitude may be imposed upon the individual by official authority under powers committed to any political organization under our Constitution. We examine rather than assume existence of this power and, against this broader definition of issues in this case, re-examine specific grounds assigned for the *Gobitis* decision. . . .

The *Gobitis* opinion reasoned that this is a field "where courts possess no marked and certainly no controlling competence," that it is committed to the legislatures as well as the courts to guard cherished liberties and that it is constitutionally appropriate to "fight out the wise use of legislative authority in the forum of public opinion and before legislative assemblies rather than to transfer such a contest to the judicial arena," since all the "effective means of inducing political changes are left free."

The very purpose of a Bill of Rights was to withdraw certain subjects from the vicissitudes of political controversy, to place them beyond the reach of majorities and officials and to establish them as legal principles to be applied by the courts. One's rights to life, liberty, and property, to free speech, a free press, freedom of worship and assembly, and other fundamental rights may not be submitted to vote; they depend on the outcome of no elections. . . .

The *Gobitis* Case Got It Wrong

Lastly, and this is the very heart of the *Gobitis* opinion, it reasons that "national unity is the basis of national security," that the authorities have "the right to select appropriate means for its attainment," and hence reaches the conclusion that such compulsory measures toward "national unity" are constitutional. Upon the verity of this assumption depends our answer in this case.

National unity as an end which officials may foster by persuasion and example is not in question. The problem is whether under our Constitution compulsion as here employed is a permissible means for its achievement.

Struggles to coerce uniformity of sentiment in support of some end thought essential to their time and country have

been waged by many good as well as by evil men. Nationalism is a relatively recent phenomenon but at other times and
places the ends have been racial or territorial security, support of a dynasty or regime, and particular plans for saving
souls. As first and moderate methods to attain unity have
failed, those bent on its accomplishment must resort to an
ever increasing severity. As governmental pressure toward
unity becomes greater, so strife becomes more bitter as to
whose unity it shall be. Probably no deeper division of our
people could proceed from any provocation than from finding
it necessary to choose what doctrine and whose program public educational officials shall compel youth to unite in em-
bracing. Ultimate futility of such attempts to compel coherence
is the lesson of every such effort from the Roman drive to
stamp out Christianity as a disturber of its pagan unity, the
Inquisition, as a means to religious and dynastic unity, the
Siberian exiles as a means to Russian unity, down to the fast
failing efforts of our present totalitarian enemies. Those who
begin coercive elimination of dissent soon find themselves
exterminating dissenters. Compulsory unification of opinion
achieves only the unanimity of the graveyard.

It seems trite but necessary to say that the First Amendment to our Constitution was designed to avoid those ends
by avoiding these beginnings. There is no mysticism in the
American concept of the State or of the nature or origin of its
authority. We set up government by consent of the governed,
and the Bill of Rights denies those in power any legal opportunity to coerce that consent. Authority here is to be controlled by public opinion, not public opinion by authority.

The case is made difficult not because the principles of its
decision are obscure but because the flag involved is our own.
Nevertheless, we apply the limitations of the Constitution
with no fear that freedom to be intellectually and spiritually
diverse or even contrary will disintegrate the social organization. To believe that patriotism will not flourish if patriotic
ceremonies are voluntary and spontaneous instead of a compulsory routine is to make an unflattering estimate of the
appeal of our institutions to free minds. We can have intellectual individualism and the rich cultural diversities that

we owe to exceptional minds only at the price of occasional eccentricity and abnormal attitudes. When they are so harmless to others or to the State as those we deal with here, the price is not too great. But freedom to differ is not limited to things that do not matter much. That would be a mere shadow of freedom. The test of its substance is the right to differ as to things that touch the heart of the existing order.

If there is any fixed star in our constitutional constellation, it is that no official, high or petty, can prescribe what shall be orthodox in politics, nationalism, religion, or other matters of opinion or force citizens to confess by word or act their faith therein. If there are any circumstances which permit an exception, they do not now occur to us.

We think the action of the local authorities in compelling the flag salute and pledge transcends constitutional limitations on their power and invades the sphere of intellect and spirit which it is the purpose of the First Amendment to our Constitution to reserve from all official control.

The decision of this Court in *Minersville School District v. Gobitis* and the holdings of those few *per curiam* decisions which preceded and foreshadowed it are overruled, and the judgment enjoining enforcement of the West Virginia Regulation is *Affirmed.*

CHAPTER FOUR

Perspectives on Religious Freedom in America

The Bill of Rights

The Separation of Church and State Is Beneficial to Religion

John M. Swomley

John M. Swomley, a member of the national board of the American Civil Liberties Union and the author of *Religion, the State, and the Schools*, argues that disestablishment— the separation of government and religion—has actually been good for both church and state. Realizing that many religious people have disagreed with court decisions, he offers eight reasons why churches should favor a stronger separation of church and state, including the fact that churches are stronger when they finance their own programs and are more successful in third world nations if they they are not specifically tied to Western governments.

The religious liberty of all necessarily requires that no church, synagogue, denomination, or combination of religious organizations have the power to direct the government, its policies, or actions other than through the process of persuading public opinion on the issues or principles they advocate.

It is also essential that the government not institute its own religious activity either as a supplement or as an alternative to the religious expression of individuals or churches and synagogues. If government officials believe private religious expression is not adequate, or that the general public needs to be exposed to state-sponsored prayer services or religious gatherings under public auspices such as in public schools or in connection with public sports events, such state activity would violate religious liberty. The mere fact of prayer authorized by law is a civil matter and therefore a secular rather than religious expression.

The use by the state (and even by secular business corporations) of religious services and symbols secularizes and profanes them. The Bank of the Holy Spirit in Lisbon, Portugal, does not differ from other banks in interest rates charged to the poor or in its employment practices. When the government takes over a religious holiday or sponsors religious displays, it endorses the appearance of religiosity without the ethical and theological substance of the religion it endorses. In this way, because government is not a community of faith, it waters down and secularizes the otherwise sacred symbols. Government sponsorship of religious services, holy days, and religious symbols is thus an additional enemy of religious liberty and of religion itself.

In democracies or republics such as the United States, government rarely engages in such violations of religious liberty because it intends to secularize or to damage religion. It does so at the request of or as the result of pressure from organized religious groups. There are religious groups that believe that the state should not be an impartial administrator of justice or promoter of the general welfare but an agency to promote the true religion, which they believe is not only Christianity, but their particular expression of Christianity. Such groups retain legal and public relations staff for the purpose of gaining government aid or government expression of their position. Although such efforts over a period of decades are often counterproductive, religious bodies have a right to engage in such activity and to hold such beliefs, as do those who oppose their sectarian proposals or who oppose all religion.

Religious liberty cannot be founded on restriction of groups seeking dominance for their doctrines or organization, or on restriction of opponents of organized religion. Such restriction is the negation of liberty. The secular state, however, is constitutionally restricted and forbidden to legislate or otherwise involve itself in religious matters. That is the genius of the American doctrine of separation of church and state and of a secular constitution. Theocratic government, or something short of it in the way of government support or endorsement of religious doctrine or institutions, is a denial of religious liberty. Only when the state is secular can it be impartial and therefore guarantee equally the liberty of all religious organizations.

Some religious groups are critical of the idea of a secular state because they believe anything secular is an enemy of religion. This assumes that complete neutrality with respect to religion is hostility. This is not the American experience; religious influence in American society and church membership has grown substantially since the adoption of a secular constitution in 1787.

Why Separation of Church and State Is Good for Religion

The following reasons summarize why churches should favor separation of church and state, which is the essence of a secular state:

(1) Separation prevents the government from determining church policy, whether directly or indirectly.

(2) Separation does not permit churches to seek special privileges from government that are denied to minority religious groups and to nonreligious citizens.

(3) Churches are healthier and stronger if they assume responsibility both for financing their own programs and for stimulating their members to accept that responsibility.

(4) By operating independently of government aid, the churches deny to government the imposition of compulsory tithes on all taxpayers, believers and nonbelievers alike. The churches thus avoid the resentment of those who do not want to be forced to contribute to churches to which they do not belong and of their own members who do not welcome being forced to contribute through government taxation.

(5) Since separation precludes financial support or special privilege from government, the churches are free to engage in prophetic criticism of the government and to work for social justice.

(6) The mission of the churches is compromised by government aid to church schools and colleges that serve chiefly

middle- and upper-class students or by government subsidy of church-sponsored homes for senior citizens of the same general economic status. Church empires are costly and require additional private funds from those who use the services, thus tending to exclude millions of poor people.

(7) Government sponsorship of religious activity, including prayer services, sacred symbols, religious festivals, and the like, tends to secularize the religious activity rather than make government more ethical or religious. Prayer at the dedication of a missile silo does not make the weapon less deadly; nor does prayer in the classroom increase respect for poor teaching or inspire good discipline.

(8) The churches' witness in other nations is greater if they are not identified with Western culture or with one or more specific governments. The Dutch Reformed Church in South Africa is identified with the white government and its apartheid policy. Judaism is identified with Israel and its Palestinian policy. The Roman Catholic church was the alter ego of the [Francisco] Franco dictatorship in fascist Spain and the [Antonio de Oliviera] Salazar dictatorship in Portugal. It is the official church in Ireland and identified with the Irish Republican Army in its war to absorb northern Ireland.

The Supreme Court's Decisions on the Separation of Church and State Are Flawed

David Barton

Many critics have argued that the Supreme Court has gone too far in its attempt to separate church and state in America. One well-known critic is David Barton, founder and president of Wallbuilders, a nonprofit group that emphasizes America's constitutional, moral, and religious foundations. He has written numerous books, created several videos, helped develop public school standards, and spoken across the country.

In the following article taken from his Web site, Barton argues that Supreme Court rulings since the early 1960s have incorrectly concluded that the First Amendment calls for a "wall of separation between church and state." He shows that Thomas Jefferson, author of this famous phrase, wanted to protect individuals from government infringement on their inalienable right to practice their religion. However, instead of protecting this right, the Supreme Court rulings have instead impinged on the right to practice religion in public. In short, the concept of "separation of church and state" is being used to the opposite effect than it was originally intended.

In 1947, in the case *Everson v. Board of Education*, the Supreme Court declared, "The First Amendment has erected a wall between church and state. That wall must be kept high and impregnable. We could not approve the slightest breach." The "separation of church and state" phrase

David Barton, "The Separation of Church and State," www.wallbuilders.com. Copyright © by Wallbuilders. Reproduced by permission.

which they invoked, and which has today become so familiar, was taken from an exchange of letters between President Thomas Jefferson and the Baptist Association of Danbury, Connecticut, shortly after Jefferson became President.

The election of Jefferson—America's first Anti-Federalist President—elated many Baptists since that denomination, by-and-large, was also strongly Anti-Federalist. This political disposition of the Baptists was understandable, for from the early settlement of Rhode Island in the 1630s to the time of the federal Constitution in the 1780s, the Baptists had often found themselves suffering from the centralization of power.

The Danbury Letter

Consequently, now having a President who not only had championed the rights of Baptists in Virginia but who also had advocated clear limits on the centralization of government powers, the Danbury Baptists wrote Jefferson a letter of praise on October 7, 1801, telling him:

> Among the many millions in America and Europe who rejoice in your election to office, we embrace the first opportunity . . . to express our great satisfaction in your appointment to the Chief Magistracy in the United States. . . . We have reason to believe that America's God has raised you up to fill the Chair of State out of that goodwill which He bears to the millions which you preside over. May God strengthen you for the arduous task which providence and the voice of the people have called you. . . . And may the Lord preserve you safe from every evil and bring you at last to his Heavenly Kingdom through Jesus Christ our Glorious Mediator.

However, in that same letter of congratulations, the Baptists also expressed to Jefferson their grave concern over the entire concept of the First Amendment, including its guarantee for "the free exercise of religion":

> Our sentiments are uniformly on the side of religious liberty: that religion is at all times and places a matter between God and individuals, that no man ought to suf-

fer in name, person, or effects on account of his religious opinions, [and] that the legitimate power of civil government extends no further than to punish the man who works ill to his neighbor. But sir, our constitution of government is not specific. . . . Therefore what religious privileges we enjoy (as a minor part of the State) we enjoy as favors granted, and not as inalienable rights.

In short, the inclusion of protection for the "free exercise of religion" in the constitution suggested to the Danbury Baptists that the right of religious expression was government-given (thus alienable) rather than God-given (hence inalienable), and that therefore the government might someday attempt to regulate religious expression. This was a possibility to which they strenuously objected—unless, as they had explained, someone's religious practice caused him to "work ill to his neighbor."

Jefferson's Writings on Church-State Relations

Jefferson understood their concern; it was also his own. In fact, he made numerous declarations about the constitutional inability of the federal government to regulate, restrict, or interfere with religious expression. For example:

No power over the freedom of religion . . . [is] delegated to the United States by the Constitution.

In matters of religion, I have considered that its free exercise is placed by the Constitution independent of the powers of the general [federal] government.

Our excellent Constitution . . . has not placed our religious rights under the power of any public functionary.

I consider the government of the United States as interdicted [prohibited] by the Constitution from intermeddling with religious institutions . . . or exercises.

Jefferson believed that the government was to be powerless to interfere with religious expressions for a very simple reason: he had long witnessed the unhealthy tendency of government to encroach upon the free exercise of religion. As he explained to Noah Webster:

It had become an universal and almost uncontroverted position in the several states that the purposes of society do not require a surrender of all our rights to our ordinary governors . . . and which experience has nevertheless proved they [the government] will be constantly encroaching on if submitted to them; that there are also certain fences which experience has proved peculiarly efficacious [effective] against wrong and rarely obstructive of right, which yet the governing powers have ever shown a disposition to weaken and remove. Of the first kind, for instance, is freedom of religion.

Thomas Jefferson had no intention of allowing the government to limit, restrict, regulate, or interfere with public religious practices. He believed, along with the other Founders, that the First Amendment had been enacted *only* to prevent the federal establishment of a national denomination—a fact he made clear in a letter to fellow-signer of the Declaration of Independence Benjamin Rush:

The clause of the Constitution which, while it secured the freedom of the press, covered also the freedom of religion, had given to the clergy a very favorite hope of obtaining an establishment of a particular form of Christianity through the United States; and as every sect believes its own form the true one, every one perhaps hoped for his own, but especially the Episcopalians and Congregationalists. The returning good sense of our country threatens abortion to their hopes and they believe that any portion of power confided to me will be exerted in opposition to their schemes. And they believe rightly.

Jefferson had committed himself as President to pursuing the purpose of the First Amendment: preventing the "establishment of a particular form of Christianity" by the Episcopalians, Congregationalists, or any other denomination.

Since this was Jefferson's view concerning religious expression, in his short and polite reply to the Danbury Baptists on January 1, 1802, he assured them that they need not fear; that the free exercise of religion would *never* be interfered with by the federal government. As he explained:

> Gentlemen,—The affectionate sentiments of esteem and approbation which you are so good as to express towards me on behalf of the Danbury Baptist Association give me the highest satisfaction. . . . Believing with you that religion is a matter which lies solely between man and his God; that he owes account to none other for his faith or his worship; that the legislative powers of government reach actions only and not opinions, I contemplate with sovereign reverence that act of the whole American people which declared that their legislature should "make no law respecting an establishment of religion or prohibiting the free exercise thereof," thus building a wall of separation between Church and State. Adhering to this expression of the supreme will of the nation in behalf of the rights of conscience, I shall see with sincere satisfaction the progress of those sentiments which tend to restore to man all his natural rights, convinced he has no natural right in opposition to his social duties. I reciprocate your kind prayers for the protection and blessing of the common Father and Creator of man, and tender you for yourselves and your religious association assurances of my high respect and esteem.

Jefferson's reference to "natural rights" invoked an important legal phrase which was part of the rhetoric of that day and which reaffirmed his belief that religious liberties were inalienable rights. While the phrase "natural rights" communicated much to people then, to most citizens today those words mean little.

By definition, "natural rights" included "that which the Books of the Law and the Gospel do contain" [as stated by sixteenth-century English theologian Richard Hooker]. That is, "natural rights" incorporated what God Himself had guaranteed to man in the Scriptures. Thus, when Jefferson assured the Baptists that by following their "natural rights" they would violate *no* social duty, he was affirming to them that the free exercise of religion was their inalienable God-given right and therefore was protected from federal regulation or interference.

So clearly did Jefferson understand the Source of America's inalienable rights that he even doubted whether America could survive if we ever lost that knowledge. He queried:

> And can the liberties of a nation be thought secure if we have lost the only firm basis, a conviction in the minds of the people that these liberties are the gift of God? That they are not to be violated but with His wrath?

Jefferson believed that God, not government, was the Author and Source of our rights and that the government, therefore, was to be prevented from interference with those rights. Very simply, the "fence" of the Webster letter and the "wall" of the Danbury letter were *not* to limit religious activities in public; rather they were to limit the power of the government to prohibit or interfere with those expressions.

Early Courts Understood Jefferson

Earlier courts long understood Jefferson's intent. In fact, when Jefferson's letter was invoked by the Supreme Court (only once prior to the 1947 *Everson* case—the *Reynolds* v. *United States* case in 1878), unlike today's Courts which publish only his eight-word separation phrase, that earlier Court published Jefferson's entire letter and then concluded:

> Coming as this does from an acknowledged leader of the advocates of the measure, it [Jefferson's letter] may be accepted almost as an authoritative declaration of the scope and effect of the Amendment thus secured. *Congress* was deprived of all *legislative power* over mere [religious] opinion, but was left free to *reach actions which were in violation of social duties or subversive of good order* (emphasis added).

That Court then succinctly summarized Jefferson's intent for "separation of church and state":

The rightful purposes of civil government are for its officers to interfere when principles break out into overt acts against peace and good order. In this . . . is found the true distinction between what properly belongs to the church and what to the State.

With this even the Baptists had agreed; for while wanting to see the government prohibited from interfering with or limiting religious activities, they also had declared it a legitimate function of government "to punish the man who works ill to his neighbor."

That Court, therefore, and others (for example, *Commonwealth* v. *Nesbit* and *Lindenmuller* v. *The People*), identified actions into which—if perpetrated in the name of religion— the government *did* have legitimate reason to intrude. Those activities included human sacrifice, polygamy, bigamy, concubinage, incest, infanticide, parricide, advocation and promotion of immorality, etc.

Such acts, even if perpetrated in the name of religion, would be stopped by the government since, as the Court had explained, they were "subversive of good order" and were "overt acts against peace." However, the government was *never* to interfere with *traditional* religious practices outlined in "the Books of the Law and the Gospel"—whether public prayer, the use of the Scriptures, public acknowledgements of God, etc.

Therefore, if Jefferson's letter is to be used today, let its context be clearly given—as in previous years. Furthermore, earlier Courts had always viewed Jefferson's Danbury letter for just what it was: a *personal, private* letter to a specific group. There is probably no other instance in America's history where words spoken by a single individual in a private letter—words clearly divorced from their context—have become the sole authorization for a national policy. Finally, Jefferson's Danbury letter should never be invoked as a stand-alone document. A proper analysis of Jefferson's views must include his numerous other statements on the First Amendment.

For example, in addition to his other statements previously noted, Jefferson also declared that the "power to prescribe any religious exercise . . . *must rest with the States*" (emphasis added). Nevertheless, the federal courts ignore this succinct declaration and choose rather to misuse his separation phrase to strike down scores of State laws which encourage or facilitate public religious expressions. Such rulings against State laws are a direct violation of the words and intent of the very one from whom the courts claim to derive their policy.

One further note should be made about the now infamous "separation" dogma. The *Congressional Records* from June 7 to September 25, 1789, record the months of discussions and debates of the ninety Founding Fathers who framed the First Amendment. Significantly, not only was Thomas Jefferson not one of those ninety who framed the First Amendment, but also, during those debates not one of those ninety Framers ever mentioned the phrase "separation of church and state." It seems logical that if this had been the intent for the First Amendment—as is so frequently asserted—then at least one of those ninety who framed the Amendment would have mentioned that phrase; none did.

In summary, the "separation" phrase so frequently invoked today was rarely mentioned by any of the Founders; and even Jefferson's explanation of his phrase is diametrically opposed to the manner in which courts apply it today. "Separation of church and state" currently means almost exactly the opposite of what it originally meant.

Americans Will Continue to Demand the Right to Religious Freedoms

Cathy Young

Cathy Young is a research associate at the Cato Institute, a libertarian public policy research foundation. In the following article she explores the clash between free speech and the free exercise of religion. She cites recent cases in which religious expression has been limited, sometimes legitimately and sometimes on dubious grounds. For example, religious expression has been prohibited simply in order to protect the listeners' sensitivities rather than to prevent the establishment of an official religion, as dictated by the Constitution. Young believes court cases over religious expression in public schools will continue as America's culturally diverse people demand to be allowed to practice their faiths publicly.

The latest round in the perennial legal battle over the separation of church and state ended on June 19 [2001], when the U.S. Supreme Court struck down a Texas school district's policy permitting voluntary, student-initiated public prayers before high school football games. But the litigation over religious expression in public schools is likely to continue. It is a conflict in which two key First Amendment protections—freedom of speech and the prohibition against state establishment of religion—seem to collide. And yet the real paradox, perhaps, is that neither side in this debate wants speech to be really free when it comes to religion.

The Supreme Court case, *Santa Fe Independent School District* v. *Doe*, began in 1995, when several families challenged the practice of having a prayer delivered over the school's public address system at the start of each home varsity football game. The plaintiffs—not atheists but Catholics and Mormons—saw this as part of a general pattern of promotion of a specific brand of Christianity by the schools of the mostly Baptist town. Teachers led prayers before lunch, handed out flyers for revival meetings, and in some cases actively proselytized students of other faiths and disparaged their beliefs.

After the lawsuit was filed, the district took steps to curb these excesses and devised an ostensibly neutral solution to the problem of public prayer at football games: The students would elect a speaker to deliver pre-game remarks—religious or secular—to "solemnize the event." It is this policy that the high court has rejected as thinly disguised public sponsorship of prayer.

In a caustic dissent, Chief Justice William Rehnquist complained that the majority opinion, written by Justice John Paul Stevens, "bristles with hostility to all things religious in public life." Yet Rehnquist conceded that if the disputed policy resulted in prayer, say, 90 percent of the time, it would probably be unconstitutional.

Conservative critics of a strict separation of church and state frame the issue as one of free speech and free exercise of religion. This emphasis is shrewd political strategy—no one wants to admit to being against either freedom—but it also raises a thorny issue. If government schools allow student-initiated religious expression at official school events, are they unconstitutionally promoting religion? If they muzzle such expression, are they unconstitutionally suppressing speech?

Even conservative Pepperdine University law professor Douglas Kmiec, who believes that modern secularism has "perverted" the constitutional ban on an official state religion into a mandate to banish religiosity from the public square, wrote in *The Wall Street Journal* that, "given the peculiar facts of the case, the Supreme Court may have been right" to strike down the Santa Fe policy. Those facts included the district's history of practices that were clearly unconstitutional even under the narrowest interpretation of the Establishment Clause. The policy allowing an elected student speaker to deliver an invocation was rather transparently designed as a way to preserve pre-game prayer.

Religious Speech Under Attack

But in other, more complex cases currently moving through the legal system, there is a far stronger claim that absolute separation unfairly singles out religious speech. Take the saga of the brothers Chris and Jason Niemeyer, devout evangelical Christians and successive class valedictorians at Oroville High School in California in 1998 and 1999. The Niemeyers were barred from giving the traditional commencement address to their classmates because they wanted to talk about their faith.

As many schools require, Chris Niemeyer gave the school administrators an advance copy of his speech, which asserted that all people are "God's children, through Jesus Christ's death, when we accept his free love and saving grace," and urged listeners to embrace a "personal relationship" with God. The principal told him to tone down the religious message. After an unsuccessful attempt to get a court order securing his right to speak, the boy wanted to make brief remarks at graduation explaining why he couldn't give a speech. But school officials stopped him on his way to the podium and told him he couldn't speak at all—a gesture that prompted loud protests from the crowd and nearly sparked a riot.

The following year, Jason Niemeyer submitted a valedictory address that, while less focused on religion, concluded by urging all those present "to take advantage of the friendship that is offered us in Christ." After consulting with attorneys, the school forbade him to give the speech and also nixed a revised version with no direct references to Jesus.

Both of the brothers are suing the school district. [As of 2001] the courts have sided with the school, which argues that graduation is an extension of the school curriculum and that, therefore, sectarian commencement messages should not be permitted.

Yet had the brothers been allowed to speak, interpreting their remarks as "establishment of religion" by the state would have been far more of a stretch than in the Texas football case. A valedictorian's address has a clear secular purpose, and neither boy would have been the sole graduation speaker. It is doubtful that any student in the audience could have perceived a religiously themed valedictory speech as official endorsement of a sectarian creed by the school (any more than Chris Niemeyer's election as class president in his senior year, at a time when he was also the co-leader of a Christian club at school, amounted to an endorsement of religion).

Protecting Feelings

To remove any shade of suspicion, an administrator could have made a statement that any expressions of religious faith reflected the speakers' individual beliefs. Indeed, the concern of the officials seems to have been less that some people would feel coerced or discriminated against than that some people would feel uncomfortable.

In a declaration filed in the legal case, Chris Niemeyer's covaledictorian, Delisa Freistadt, who is Jewish, stated that she was glad the court didn't "force" her to listen to his speech. The Niemeyers' attorneys counter, rather persuasively, that it is part of the American way that we are sometimes forced to listen to speech we don't like. (Freistadt could have countered speech with more speech and used her time at the podium to talk about respecting religious differences.) As applied in this case so far, the First Amendment seems to be less a guarantee of religious freedom than a speech code guaranteeing that no one's feelings are hurt.

There may be an anti-religion double standard at work as well. Some of the Niemeyers' local supporters gripe that the same school officials who muzzled the boys allowed the installation of a Vietnam War mural many people found objectionable. It also seems likely that if a public school had silenced a valedictorian who wanted to praise vegetarianism or assail racism, the mainstream media and the American Civil Liberties Union would have blasted the decision as an outrageous act of censorship.

The ACLU has criticized the free speech defense of student-initiated prayer at graduation, cautioning that such a position would force schools to grant equal access to all speakers of all viewpoints on a first come, first served basis—a less relevant concern when the issue is one of free expression for speakers already chosen on an ideologically neutral basis. It is also worth noting that the Colorado ACLU has championed the right of black students to wear a ceremonial African cloth over their graduation gowns as a protected form of expression.

An even better case that strict separationism can turn into censorship can be made in a suit currently pending in the U.S. Court of Appeals for the 3rd Circuit in Philadelphia, brought by the parents of Medford, New Jersey, schoolboy Zachary Hood. In 1996, each child in the boy's first-grade public school class was asked to choose a story to read aloud. Zachary's selection, the story of the reconciliation between the brothers Jacob and Esau from *The Beginner's Bible*, was deemed inappropriate by the teacher, even though it contained no mention of God or miracles. He was told that he could read it to her in private but not to the entire class.

In 1999 a three-judge panel of the 3rd Circuit ruled that the teacher acted properly, agreeing with the school's rather wobbly argument that permitting the story to be read in the classroom would have sent a message to the impressionable kiddies that "the teacher or the school endorsed the Bible." Late [in 2000], however, the full court vacated that decision and agreed to consider the case, which may go all the way to the Supreme Court.

It would be difficult to dispute the religious conservatives' claim that the treatment of Zachary Hood or of the Niemeyers reflects "viewpoint discrimination" against religious speech. It is fairly clear that in these instances it is the exclusion rather than the inclusion of religion that may "discriminate against, or oppress, a particular sect or religion," as Justice William Brennan put it in the 1963 ruling *School District of Abington v. Schempp*, which found mandatory school prayer unconstitutional.

Religion Is Not Treated as Any Other Viewpoint

But it would also be disingenuous for the anti-secularists to claim that they want religion to be treated as just another viewpoint in the marketplace of ideas—a viewpoint which can be defended but can also be attacked and even ridiculed, like any other idea. Indeed, the same people who wax poetic about defending religious liberty for Christians can get very unhappy with the wrong kind of speech about religion. Just as religious conservatives now couch their demands for prayer in public schools in the "liberal" language of free speech, their attempts to squelch what used to be called sacrilege are couched in the politically correct language of anti-bigotry and opposition to "hate speech." The charge of "Christian bashing" (or "Catholic bashing") has been directed, for instance, at the ABC show *Nothing Sacred*, which questioned Catholic doctrine on birth control and priestly celibacy.

In 1998 news of a Broadway production of Terrence McNally's play *Corpus Christi*, depicting a gay Jesus-like character, sparked a predictable firestorm. The Catholic League for Religious and Civil Rights launched a letter-writing campaign demanding that the production be canceled. It is true, of course, that a protest is not censorship. But when the Manhattan Theater Club decided to cancel the play due to threats of violence and arson, the Catholic League's jubilant reaction did not show a strong commitment to free speech. While formally deploring the threats, the league warned that if another company picked up *Corpus Christi*, it would "wage a war that no one will forget." (The theater eventually revived the production after coming under fire from the press and from authors.) Catholic League President William Donohue explicitly, and favorably, compared the anti–*Corpus Christi* protests to the actions taken by racial, ethnic, and feminist groups against speech they find offensive.

And in July [2001], in what may be the most creative use of hate speech phraseology to date, L. Brent Bozell's Media Research Center ran an ad accusing CBS of "condoning religious bigotry." *Early Show* host Bryant Gumbel had been caught on camera saying "What a ——ing idiot!" after an interview with the Family Research Council's Robert Knight, who had defended on religious grounds the Boy Scouts' exclusion of gays. Even if Gumbel was referring to Knight and not, as some have claimed, to a CBS staffer, it is noteworthy that he used no slurs referring to Knight's faith. (Is it racist to call Al Sharpton a flicking idiot?) Nonetheless, Bozell invoked CBS' firing of sports oddsmaker Jimmy "The Greek" Snyder for televised comments about the innate racial superiority of black athletes and concluded that "racial bigotry on CBS is dealt with unequivocally; religious bigotry on CBS is met with a disinterested yawn."

Protecting Sensitivities

In an essay published in *The New York Times Magazine* last January [2001], legal commentator Jeffrey Rosen noted that the strict separationism endorsed by the courts in the early 1970s, which held that the government could not support any religious activity in any form, has given way to "a very different constitutional principle that demands equal treatment for religion." Under this doctrine, Bible study clubs and prayer groups can function on public school property on a par with other student groups, and parochial schools can receive federal aid for special education programs on a par with other schools. (School vouchers that would subsidize tuition at religious schools remain a more contentious issue.)

Rosen insightfully links the crumbling of the wall between church and state to the rise of cultural diversity: "In an era when religious identity now competes with race, sex and ethnicity as a central aspect of how Americans define themselves, it seems like discrimination—the only unforgivable sin in a multicultural age—to forbid people to express their religious beliefs in an increasingly fractured public sphere." As Rosen concludes, the resulting expansion of freedom of religious expression may well be a healthy development for public life. But the examples of race and sex also point to certain dangers. While the new appreciation of diversity can liberate discussion and expression, it can just as easily narrow the range of acceptable speech in order to protect sensitivities.

The Origins of the American Bill of Rights

The U.S. Constitution as it was originally created and submitted to the colonies for ratification in 1787 did not include
what we now call the Bill of Rights. This omission was the
cause of much controversy as Americans debated whether to
accept the new Constitution and the new federal government
it created. One of the main concerns voiced by opponents of
the document was that it lacked a detailed listing of guarantees of certain fundamental individual rights. These critics
did not succeed in preventing the Constitution's ratification,
but were in large part responsible for the existence of the
Bill of Rights.

In 1787 the United States consisted of thirteen former
British colonies that had been loosely bound since 1781 by
the Articles of Confederation. Since declaring their independence from Great Britain in 1776, the former colonies
had established their own colonial governments and constitutions, eight of which had bills of rights written into them.
One of the most influential was Virginia's Declaration of
Rights. Drafted largely by planter and legislator George
Mason in 1776, the seventeen-point document combined
philosophical declarations of natural rights with specific limitations on the powers of government. It served as a model
for other state constitutions.

The sources for these declarations of rights included English law traditions dating back to the 1215 Magna Carta
and the 1689 English Bill of Rights—two historic documents
that provided specific legal guarantees of the "true, ancient,
and indubitable rights and liberties of the people" of England. Other legal sources included the colonies' original char-
ters, which declared that colonists should have the same
"privileges, franchises, and immunities" that they would if
they lived in England. The ideas concerning natural rights